MW00893178

Congregational Connections

SWPA Synod Resource Center
9625 Perry Highway
Pittsburgh, PA 15237

Congregational Connections

*Uniting Six Generations
in the Church*

Carroll Anne Sheppard
and Nancy Burton Dilliplane,
Contributing Author

Library of Congress Control Number: 2011913452
ISBN: Hardcover   978-1-4653-4447-2
               Softcover   978-1-4653-4446-5
               Ebook   978-1-4653-4448-9

This book was printed in the United States of America.

To order additional copies of this book, contact:
Xlibris Corporation
1-888-795-4274
www.Xlibris.com
Orders@Xlibris.com
102186

Contents

It starts here:

A Congregational Moment

Pastor GenX told us he had recently conducted a funeral service for one of the former congregational leaders, a man who was deeply loved and respected. His wife used to run the Funeral Hospitality Guild, which provided refreshments in the Church Hall after the service for family and friends. Now her time of need had come, and she was too frail and too devastated by her loss for anyone to think that she would organize the reception. Unfortunately, all of her peers were also too old or had moved away into retirement homes or other states to be with their children. Somehow, no one had realized that the Funeral Guild members had left, one by one, until there was almost no one who could perform this ministry.

Pastor GenX took the issue to the Church Board which was meeting the following evening. After he described the situation, Erin, who ran a part-time catering business from her house, said that she could help out. Everyone heaved a sigh of relief. The reception was lovely. The food and drink was just right, and many people complimented Erin. Pastor GenX was also grateful.

Then Erin sent the widow a bill.

Something new is happening in America's mainline churches. It is not the return of a trend that has happened before, although some patterns may look similar. It is unprecedented in human experience. This is the first time in the world's history when significant numbers of six demographic cohorts have all occupied the stage at the same time. (*Cohort* is a term demographers use to describe those born within a certain time period. It also is used by marketers to describe those who have certain characteristics in common, as well as shared birth years.) The problem with this, put very simply, is this: none of us have a clue how to live in a six-generational cohort society!

What is intensifying the problem is that these six generational cohorts are trying to squeeze themselves into an outdated three-generation model of elders, households raising children/career singles, and children. Whether this old model is actually true or perceived as true, many organizations still operate as though it was true. Most churches do. And they certainly do not know how to manage four active adult cohorts, plus the oldest elders and the youngest children, at the same time.

For most of American history, the Grandparents-Parents-and-Children model has been a good guide to basic organization. While the mythical family of Norman Rockwell's Thanksgiving may never have really existed, and some families enjoyed the presence of great-grandparents, except for times of war three generations at a time was our most common experience.

Trying to fit six generations into three slots is proving difficult. Some social institutions are proving flexible enough to take the strain, such as community or neighborhood organizations. Social networks are creating new structures that seem to help. Many others are finding it more difficult to sort out expectations, roles and responsibilities. This includes many of our traditional mainline Protestant congregations, as well as some Catholic and Jewish congregations. Their clergy and lay leaders are finding today's reality very hard to deal with.

Our Moment of Revelation

We, Nancy and Carroll, had suspected that things were changing on the generational front for more than a year. We had spoken with a number of clergy in a study group about GenXers, and Carroll had worked with Congregational Boards and their leaders on generational issues for two years. But the day when we heard Pastor GenX talk about the Funeral Guild incident in his congregation, we knew that the congregational world had morphed into something different.

Erin, a professional working from home, is acting on her understanding of how the world works. The widow and her friends have a different understanding of the unwritten rules of society. Clergy and parish leaders need to understand what demographic cohorts are, and why communication between them is so difficult, before they can begin to sort out what is happening in their congregations. And they need to know—soon!

The Six Generational Cohorts

Look at the following chart that names each of the six cohorts. While the names vary according to author and academic discipline, they sort themselves out fairly clearly. There will probably be continuing disagreement about exactly which years mark the dividing line between them, and for our purposes, it does not matter very much. What is much more important to this discussion is that several of these cohorts are trying to play traditional roles and do not understand why the other(s) won't move aside or play by their rules.

Demographic Cohort Definitions

Age Ranges in 2011	Approximate Birth Years	Demographic and Popular Names	Referred to in the text:
110-87	1901-1924	Builders	*These*
86-69/66	1925-1942(45)*	Silents	*Cohorts*
68/65-51/48	1943(46)-1960(63)**	(Baby) Boomers	*Are "Olders"*
51/48-30/27	1960(63)-1981(84)	Gen X; (Baby) Busters Survivors;	These
26/29-11	1982(85)-2001***	Millennials Mosaics; Gen Y; Baby Boomlet	Cohorts
10-	2001-2020?	Gen Z?	Are "Youngers"

* End of WW II ** Kennedy assassination—1963
*** 9/11

At the same time that new cohorts are being added like successive mountain ranges being thrown up by tectonic plate action, other global forces are sweeping across them.

Technology and worldview are accelerating the pressures that the six generational cohorts are putting on our society. They are creating a generational divide as they reorder the way in which we live our daily lives.

The electronic revolution is changing the way we think and act. The younger the person is, the more likely that they use electronic technology and are comfortable with it. Indeed, those born after 1980 regard electronic media and the Internet as foundational to their experience of the world. The older the person is, the less likely that they use electronic era technology, texting and social networking on a daily basis.

The other factor is worldview. Boomers and those older than they were raised by people who had experienced global warfare and the ordering mechanisms connected with it. Those born after 1970—with some exceptions—were not raised by people with direct experience of global warfare. The American draft was discontinued in 1973.

These two forces, technology and worldview shift, are adding another quantum level of stress to organizations already feeling deeply pressured by six generational cohorts squeezing into three expected roles. Nowhere is this more obvious than in our traditional churches. For them, it is causing a confusing, exciting, anxiety- and conflict-producing mess.

How do the six cohorts function in congregational life?

The oldest cohort, the Builders, is nearly legendary. Tom Brokaw has not called them "The Greatest Generation" for nothing. The oldest fought as youngsters in World War I; they lived through the Great Depression; and they led this country through World War II. They had a presence and power in most congregations that still resonates. They were the "captains of industry" in the fifties and sixties who created the industrial might America enjoyed. Their world was segmented and top-down. They continue to work and provide order and stability to their congregations and families as long as they are physically and mentally able. A growing number are living and functioning well late into their nineties.

Silents mostly let the Builders have their way, for they were trained to "put up and shut up" while their elders got on with saving the world. Boomers experienced Builders as parents and grandparents who respected authority and expected order. Now Silents and Boomers expect to step into Builder roles as elders, tradition bearers and governors of their congregations. For the most part, they share similar expectations about how the church should be structured, and it is largely based on the Builder model. Many active Builders still hold the financial and patriarchal/matriarchal reins of power, even if they have retired from active leadership roles.

Boomers are pretty sure that they introduced most of the real changes in the world, and made new rules for themselves again and again. The numerically largest cohort in history until the Millennials, they have had a very large influence on popular culture. But they are beginning to lose their center-stage position. Many are frustrated that The Great Recession and global power shifts have changed their plans for retirement, delaying or threatening it. Many watch with envy the Silents who have already retired in apparent comfort. Many are horrified that they are now seen as "older workers" when so many Silents are still active in the workplace. Others are ready to accept the "Older" designation, but wonder why the respect and status they expected as elders, seems to have gone away. Boomers are not feeling as special as they once did, but they have worked and waited for the top-dog role for a long time, and they are looking hard for it.

Those born after 1970, south of the worldview shift and technology divide, often do not see the reason for the much of what older cohorts do and want them to do. If they care about attending worship, they may not care about committing to governance and continuing traditions. They may care little about maintaining buildings and structures they did not erect, and which seem to support a worldview they do not share.

While people in every cohort are economically stressed, many GenXers are particularly vulnerable. The burden of The Great Recession and its subsequent global aftershocks in European economies has fallen heavily on them, with fewer jobs, less work available, large debts and often, a mortgage that exceeds the current value of their house. GenX often responds with cynicism and sarcasm to a world that never lived up to the one older generations promised them. GenX takes its considerable initiative to the sports world or new technology businesses. Many are single; many are in partnered rather than married relationships; and they along with the married may be raising children.

Older Millennials, who are just emerging from the classroom, are meeting economic reality with disbelief, but have been warned all their lives that finding a job and making a living may not be easy. Many are continuing to live at home, by choice or by necessity. They spend large amounts of time in the electronic world with real or virtual friends and avatars. They often text or tweet each other even when in a face-to-face environment.

We don't know what GenZ will be like yet, but they certainly won't resemble Builders or Boomers. They are present in many traditional worship settings, but often not appreciated by older members unless they are related to them. Increasingly, they are moved with their parents into a niche worship service where more informal singing and prayers are common.

What happens in Congregations?

In the past, most churches could depend on a group of elders who carried on traditions and governed the congregation, younger adults who did the work and raised the children, and the children themselves. In many cases, three generations represented continuing families, but singles as well as family units without parents or children could find a place somewhere in these age-graded groups.

In the six-generational cohort society, it is often unclear who is in charge, who will do the work, and who is raising the children. Even describing this mess is confusing! Only the children seem recognizable as a group, and the older ones may already function as adults within the electronic world. Because there are so many people between 15 and 85 functioning in the two traditional adult roles of elder and worker, role confusion abounds. Those between 15 and 85 may even occupy both the elder and worker role simultaneously. In the six-cohorts-in-three-social-roles confusion, it may also be unclear which is the cause of the challenge and which is the effect. Is the problem for congregations: six cohorts; or is it three traditional roles?

Simultaneously, the generational divides, marked by age, worldview and technology, are slowly depleting congregations of attendance and support. The Olders (Builders, Silents and Boomers) may be frustrated and struggling to understand what is happening to "their church"; the Youngers (GenX and Millennials) are trying to find God, community, and raise their children in a world increasingly hostile to denominational religion. As Gordon MacDonald describes so well in his 2007 book, *Who Stole My Church?* even attempting to discuss the issues that mark the generational divide may cause conflict and emotional distress. Boomers and GenXers often form the front lines in the generational skirmishes.

Yet some congregations seem to be thriving. Those with stable multi-generational attendance, (especially when these are family groupings linked through multiple generations,) are working out ways of dealing with the issues that arise. Family loyalty may bridge tensions and permit younger members to embrace newer music and technology in their worship. (Think of the way Thanksgiving celebrations have changed within extended families, yet have been able to continue, to get an idea of how this process works.) At the same time, households and extended families may have acculturated their younger members in traditional worship and music, so these patterns and songs are familiar to them. Christmas is an example of such widely shared multi-generational traditions. Yet even the strongest family and community gatherings may experience challenges related to new technology and shifting worldview.

Other congregations may find themselves with increasingly more members on one side of the generational divide or the other. Leaders may be mostly born before 1960, or mostly afterward. Where GenXers have achieved critical mass, Boomers may largely be missing. Then the Silents and few attending Builders may form a natural group of elders, provided that they are willing to accept very different music, leadership styles and worship patterns. Or the reverse may happen, and the Boomers may largely populate the congregation, with few GenXers present. The Boomers may try to move into the "elder" slot and will hold most of the seats on the Board, but still be the workers. And having worked a long time to earn the board seat, they will not willingly or easily give it up. In this case, Boomers will try hard to get any GenXers in the congregation to pick up the committee and building work, and be resentful that there are no volunteers.

Growing concerns about financial support, children's spiritual formation and maintenance of buildings worry congregational boards and clergy. Regularly scheduled committee meetings, the staple of face-to-face communication of the Boomer/Silent world, and annual congregational events seem to lack committed support. Younger people take turns attending worship, and regard once-a-month attendance (often when a member of their household has an assigned Sunday task) as active membership.

It just isn't working the way the old three-generation model worked!

In the following pages, we will explore how we got here, both in terms of American society and of church congregations. The demographic and generational cohort insights of a number of authors will offer further insights on why misunderstandings are rife.

Chapter One will explore some of the forces that created our new six-cohort society. Then Chapter Two will look at some of the characteristics of each cohort, especially as it affects congregational experiences.

In Chapter Three, we look toward the future. We will seek to understand the generational divide that separates those fifty-and-over (Olders) from those forty-and-under (Youngers), and the important role our forty-to-fifty year olds can play as translators, bridges and peace makers. Chapter Four will examine realities for congregational life in the early 21st century. Some simple exercises may help sharpen clergy and Board members' understanding of the challenges inherent in dealing with a six-generation society. From Chapter Four onward, we will use "Congregational Moments" like the one that opened this book to help understand what these issues look like in human terms.

Chapters Five and Six will focus our attention at Worship and Christian Formation. Liturgy and Christian education—in the broadest sense—offer powerful ways to rebuild community when programs and buildings stop drawing younger adults. Chapter Seven deals with programs. We will talk about space usage and maintenance throughout Chapters Five through Seven. Chapter Eight will discuss 21st century church—where community counts more than Sunday worship statistics.

In the closing chapter, we will explore opportunities for hope and the ways in which congregational leaders can begin to invent ways of "being church" when the old ways of "doing church" are less and less productive. Frank assessment of congregational patterns and generational realities will be part of the discernment process we are all engaged in as we try to learn how to live as Christians in the six-generation society.

Our challenge will be to find ways both to minister to different segments of our congregations and to assert the simple truth that we are all children of God, in this together. We as church leaders need to find some good answers and solutions quickly, because extended lifetimes, more rapid cohort formation, and flatter communication networks suggest that anyone born in the first part of the 21st century may well experience during their lifetime what it is like to live in the first eight-cohort society.

Chapter One

How We Got Here

Several decades ago, it seemed that the Biblical grant of three score years and ten was about right. We would ideally live reasonably healthy lives for about 70 years and then experience one or more nearly fatal illnesses, grow feeble and die within the next two decades. A few would live well for longer times, mostly because they had "good genes" that would extend their lives, perhaps even to 90 or 100. But no one would survive much beyond that.

Today we are looking at the possibility of far more extended lifetimes. Teaching hospitals and research centers are growing replacement organs from a person's own organic tissues, ready for surgeons to implant without fear of the body's rejection. Repairs are being made with microsurgery so that tiny vessels and very small openings are used for the restoration of health. Personally-customized drugs are being developed as you read this.

The day of routine personal genotyping is not far off. When that happens, drugs and therapies will begin to be personalized, adapted for our own particular genetic background and needs. It will be crude to begin with, but increasingly focused, as drugs are used selectively to match our bodies' requirements.

What does this mean for tomorrow?

First of all, it means that we will not have a long old age. If most of what debilitates us and interferes with our enjoyment of life is removed, we will spend much longer in the "middle stage" of our lives—vigorous adulthood. The old notion of middle age, which had to do with a time when one's children matured enough to function in the adult world, is gone. Instead, children now mature while their parents are completing their first career and are ready after 20 or 25 years to move on to another. Then parents and children may suddenly be competing for entry level jobs.

Adults are now experiencing multiple "middle stages" rather than middle age. Boomers are coping with two middle stages, and many have changed careers in their forties or early fifties, having already spent 20 or 25 years in their first. (The Great Recession has abetted this through layoffs and downsizings.) Before too many more years pass, if the trend toward longer lifetimes accelerates, several "middle stages" and multiple careers will be common. When that happens, both parents and children may be competing with grandchildren for those same entry-level positions.

In the face of this increase in the number of persons seeking entry-level positions, young people may respond by either seizing opportunity or retreating from the work world. They may begin working at the things they love while in high school (some already have e-business ventures before graduating), and continue to explore those realms as they create and take jobs in entrepreneurial businesses. But often they come home, needing family and support before they move with any confidence into employment. The old saw: "You can't get a job without experience" is a harsh reality for our Youngers in an economy that has mid-lifers competing for the same jobs. Yet it is also abundantly clear to anyone with close connections to our youngest GenXers and oldest Millennials that they have a profoundly different perspective on the world than do those born before 1970. They approach this challenge with electronic tools and a team-and-project-based workstyle their Builder, Silent and Boomer predecessors do not have.

The shifting worldview mentioned in the Introduction has come about primarily through changes in American technology, history and lifestyle.

Those who are now over the age of fifty, were raised by people who had experienced the personal and societal discipline of global war. Their parents and grandparents had lived through the realities and horrors of World War I. Only 25 years later, all the young men were drafted into World War II. Food (like meat) and many simple luxuries (like gasoline) were rationed. Women learned how to run factories and perform a far greater range of industrial tasks than their mothers had. The whole population of the United States understood and participated in public silence ("Loose lips sink ships") about the war effort. The at-home population understood and abided by the top-down discipline required to win the war, because the lives of "our boys" and the men of their fathers' generation literally depended upon it. Those that lived through such discipline and won the war, raised their Boomer children with this worldview firmly in place—because it had worked. It was a given.

A focus on individual independence (think World War II Victory garden) has been replaced by team-style (think community garden and school project garden.)

Those born since 1970 in the United States have experienced a world essentially at peace, although the war talk has been nearly constant. But those wars have been fought in regions quite far away from the USA. After the Cuban missile crisis, all other military engagements were at least hundreds, if not thousands of miles distant from American shores. There has been no draft in this country since 1973, and the top-down discipline that went with the draft and mandatory service has seemed less and less admirable to young people raised in a world of relatively great safety and easy communication.

In 1969, Americans landed on the moon. It was a turning point: the view of Planet Earth from space showed the isolated unity of a single planet. " They" have turned out to be "us" in the decades afterward. Since that time, increased population mobility and instantaneous global communication have rapidly changed our work and home lives. Our Youngers do think globally—and ecology, sustainability and real-time news are part of their worldview.

Those born after 1970 inhabit a world where friends and family commonly live and work hundreds or thousands of miles away, and yet are linked by electronic communication into a 24/7 presence. CAT scans done in the US in the evening are interpreted by radiologists in Australia; banking transactions are processed in India while Americans sleep. Along with these changes, there has come into being a global electronic network that brings instantaneous video and voice transmission, globe-spanning travel available to many, and routine interaction with those of other cultures. Inter-denominational marriages no longer are worth comment; inter-ethnic, intra-gender, and inter-racial marriages, civil unions and partnerships are now common. Most Americans now work regularly with those of strikingly different backgrounds, even if they increasingly live in like-minded communities.

There have been great changes in child-bearing and child-rearing practices as the second middle-stage has extended healthy adulthood.

Many younger Boomers and GenXers have delayed childbearing until their late thirties or early forties. Late adoptions have become common. Many Boomer men are involved in second marriages with GenX women, and are just having children. Boomer gay and lesbian partners are raising children, who may be thirty or more years younger than they are. Single GenX moms may choose not to marry because they have jobs paying enough to support a child or children themselves, and don't see any reason to marry their child/children's father(s). Others have used sperm banks and in-vitro methods to have children. These varieties of lifestyle challenge traditional congregational norms. None of these things match the experience of those congregations whom Martin Luther King called the most segregated communities in America. Such churches' homogeneity of race, ethnicity and worldview gives them few tools to understand why they are experiencing reduced attendance and seem to be unattractive to many younger people. The differences in lifestyle, worldview, communication technology and work experiences noted above often have not penetrated the traditional three-generational role model in mainline Christian denominations.

Congregational leaders who are coping with these massive changes have every right to feel confused, as the pace of change accelerates. Many clergy have been trained in seminaries whose curricula changed little since the 1970's, using technologies and teaching methods that reinforce the old top-down structures. Clergy ask themselves:

"Why doesn't my training work?"

"Why do I feel as though I am constantly translating between the generations?"

"Why don't the older members understand?"

"Why don't the younger members stay?"

"Why doesn't anyone want to work or volunteer?"

"Why are our traditional programs now almost unsustainable?"

Such questions will lead us on to Chapters Two and Three, as we seek to understand why Older and Younger cohorts just don't seem to get along. But it will be useful to look at congregational dynamics first. What are these disagreements about?

Leaders may experience their own congregations as split, if peace and growth have come at the expense of one or more generational cohorts' presence. Some congregations have worked out a new version of the three-generation church by omission.

In the face of these changes, congregations, especially those with matriarchs and patriarchs from the Silent cohort, may become stubbornly passive and resistant to very different expectations brought by younger or non-traditional members. At the same time, congregational leaders observe that many GenXers (and those whose children and work environments move them into this cohort's lifestyles) are themselves passively resistant to the old church model. They are seeking something else. And no amount of marketing evangelism will get many of them into an alien three-generational church environment where they are expected to be the workers who carry on (to them) meaningless traditions. This impasse can disappear when Boomers fill the leadership roles and reinforce them in the names of their Builder and Silent parents. But such behavior may lead to GenXers' absence, and most Millennials disappear as soon as they enter college or leave home for skilled employment. There are just too many cohorts trying to occupy the two traditional adult roles!

Of course, there will always be congregational leaders in every generational cohort who see opportunity and need for change. There will always be individuals with initiative and vision, and Gen X is filled with them, especially in the new technologies companies. They in turn, may be mystified by the resistance of older congregational leaders to change.

Longer lives, generations interacting in unprecedented ways as six generational cohorts try to play on the same stage, changing social rules and demographic changes still do not tell the whole story. Because simultaneously with these shifts, the global economy tanked.

While modern economists and some brilliant players around the world used the tools that the Great Depression taught us, and some national markets like India and China seemed incredibly resilient and buoyed the global economy, we have and will experience something that echoes the Great Depression in worrisome ways. State and local governments once again are under staggering financial stress, as they (mostly) must bring in balanced budgets. Only the federal government can keep printing money whether or not there is anything of value to back it up. The resultant rise in oil and commodity prices and increase in stock prices based on the devaluation of the US currency will last as long as the rest of the world is willing to float Bank USA. Simultaneously foreclosures and bankruptcies exert strong deflationary pressures.

As the global monetary and credit storm plays out, the generational cohort pressure will be high, until we learn how to find appropriate and rewarding roles for active workforce participants from ages 15 to 85.

Not surprisingly, our first middle-stage adults (GenXers and the youngest Boomers) are worried, as they discover that millions of them own houses they purchased with a large mortgage for more than the market will now pay them for the same property. The youngest also still have school debts in amounts that Olders find hard to comprehend, and many have credit card debts at usurious rates.

The second middle-stage adults, mid and older Boomers and the youngest Silents, are also worried, as they find themselves owning properties and holding stocks and retirement accounts worth significantly less than their retirement dreams suggested would be the case. Even seemingly secure annuities, if they were based on current interest rates, have dropped hugely in their promises of retirement payouts. Many are facing the fact that they will be working—at least to pay medical coverage—for most of their remaining years. Many are well and hearty, and see no reason to leave the workforce. Modern medicine provides cures or at least accommodations with diseases that killed their grandparents in their 50's and 60's. As we noted above, this crowds the job-market and places greater obstacles for employment in the paths of younger job-seekers.

Both of these groups are also by American historical standards disproportionately involved in raising children, grandchildren, step-children, and adopted children. The world of active adults is flattening and getting age-broader. It now stretches from the teenage mother to the 70-year old raising children who is also caring for a frail elder.

These are the very people who may find a congregation to be a community of support. Those who want their children raised into and educated about Christian core values will come seeking worship and formation assistance. Those with exhausting caregiver responsibilities may be seeking communities of healing for themselves and their loved ones. Workers who find the electronic world curiously unsatisfying may come to find their first experience of inter-generational community and service. Those raised with little experience of liturgy or formal worship may be looking for intentional practice with others that deepens their sense of presence to God.

Congregational leaders are faced with having to be all things to each of the six generational cohorts: Builders, Silents, Boomers, GenXers, Millennials and the young "GenZers." Leaders themselves may come to recognize that they also share characteristics with their own cohort that may make understanding other cohorts difficult. There are few sources of training in how to recognize and deal with inter-cohort issues.

Large congregations wealthy enough to have multiple clergy and staff to minister separately to each cohort may use a successful strategy of separation and niche worship services and programs. Small congregations may be held together by extended family ties. But the many congregations in the middle-size ranks are struggling to understand an environment that is almost incomprehensible, and that seems to have arrived with little warning. In the following pages, we'll examine each of the cohorts briefly and some theories on how they are interacting.

We suggest that you spend some time with the following questions to help you make sense of the many terms and concepts we have introduced in Chapter One.

Questions:

1) Which cohort was I born into? (Look at the table opposite to help you answer this.)

2) Which cohort was I raised in? Are all my siblings older or younger than I am? Did other personal lifestyle issues move me into a different cohort's lifestyle than most of my age group?

3) Which cohort were my parents born into? My children? How many cohorts are represented in my household? At my workplace?

4) Which cohorts are present in my congregation? Which cohorts do our congregational leaders belong to?

5) How many cohorts do I interact with on a daily basis? Which cohorts don't I interact with regularly?

Demographic Cohort Definitions

Age Ranges in 2011	Approximate Birth Years	Demographic and Popular Names	Referred to in the text:
110-87	1901-1924	Builders	*These*
86-69/66	1925 - 1942(45)*	Silents	*Cohorts*
68/65-50/51	1943(46)- 1960(63)**	(Baby) Boomers	*Are "Olders"*
50/48-27/30	1961(63)- 1981(84)	Gen X; (Baby) Busters Survivors;	**These**
26/29-11	1982(85)- 2001***	Millennials Mosaics; Gen Y; Baby Boomlet	**Cohorts**
10-	2001-2020?	Gen Z?	**Are "Youngers"**

* End of WW II ** Kennedy assassination
*** 9/11

Chapter Two

Six Different Cohort Experiences

As we have seen in Chapter One, the confluence of six generational cohorts in a single society is unprecedented. No wonder we are struggling to find places for everyone and figure out how we should all get along together! The fact that the Boomer cohort is especially large in terms of sheer numbers, followed by a much smaller GenX cohort, followed by another even larger Millennial cohort is just going to make the working-out process more challenging.

As Silent and older Boomer senior clergy retire, their places will be taken by younger Boomer and GenX clergy who were trained in the old three-generation model (Elders, Worker-Bees raising children, and Children) but who—themselves, by necessity—function in many ways like those under forty. They will be asked to be translators, peacemakers, and bridges for their congregations. All congregational leaders will need to know and understand the generational cohorts' differences to be able to accurately assess what is going on when conflicts arise or members are angry and frustrated that their expectations are unfulfilled. As the oldest Millennials take clergy positions, such challenges may intensify. The temptation to take these emotionally difficult transitions personally is large. But they are symptomatic of a social ecology that is deeply stressed by macro-changes.

To the Olders, it looks as though the churches and buildings they and their parents built with hard-earned money and hours of time, are being disregarded and abandoned by the Youngers. To the Youngers, the music and programs and perhaps even worship forms that the traditional congregation embraces look irrelevant to their own sense of spirituality.

The very administrative structure of the congregation may seem top-down and unfriendly to them. They do not have the time, interest or energy to continue to support them. What is happening?

It is time to take a much closer look at the characteristics of the six cohorts. However, since we want to return to the concerns of congregations and their leaders, these sketches will be relatively brief. And as such, they may seem superficial or stereotypical—especially for your own cohort. At the end of this chapter are suggestions for further reading that will give you much more information, from a variety of perspectives, about the cohorts' lifestyles, expectations and experiences.

Here's our generational cohort grid again for easy reference.

Demographic Cohort Definitions

Age Ranges in 2011	Approximate Birth Years	Demographic and Popular Names	Referred to in the text:
110-87	1901-1924	Builders	*These*
86-69/66	1925-1942(45)*	Silents	*Cohorts*
68/65-51/48	1943(46)-1960(63)**	(Baby) Boomers	*Are "Olders"*
51/48-27/30	1961-1981(84)	Gen X; (Baby) Busters Survivors;	These
26/28-11	1982(85)-2001***	Millennials Mosaics; Gen Y; Baby Boomlet	Cohorts
10-	2001-2020?	Gen Z?	Are "Youngers"

* End of WW II ** Kennedy assassination—1963
*** 9/11

A note on leading-edge and trailing edge cohort characteristics

Social scientists have noted that each cohort has two halves: the leading edge group, who are born in the first half of the year range, and the trailing edge, born in the later half. The closer a person is to one of these edges, the more they may be influenced by the characteristics of the adjacent cohort. If, for instance, you are the youngest in a family all born in an earlier cohort, you may well have been raised as part of that cohort. Equally, if you are the oldest sibling or cousin in an extended family that identifies more with a following cohort, you may well feel as though that is your own identity, too.

If you want to read more about this topic, look for *One Church, Four Generations* by Gary L. McIntosh in the Bibliography.

The Six Cohorts: Brief Sketches

These quick sketches can offer only reminders of the historical and social reality that different cohorts experienced. They are inevitably limited, and may well be wrong for any individual person. Having said that, however, we hope you will find them useful in helping to create a mental picture for yourself of why these cohorts are identified by demographers and marketers as distinctive groups. Please also remember that any two people may have more in common because of their own life circumstances than such social analysis breakdowns would suggest. It is also important to remember that strong ethnic or cultural ties may greatly moderate cohort characteristics.

Builders—born 1901-1924

An American child born in 1901 entered a world that still greatly resembled the 19th century. Electric lights and telephones were just appearing in the homes of wealthier families in urban areas. Gaslights and oil lamps were turned on when it grew dark in cities. The sound of horse-drawn wagons, delivery vans and trams competed with the strange occasional sound of the motor car. On farms, rural areas and the frontier, life was hard and more basic. There, oil or kerosene lamps gave light. Goods moved by wagon, railroad and ship. News traveled by telegraph. Most workers worked 6 day weeks, 12 hours a day—except when they worked more. Only the well-off bathed more than once a week, and if a house was centrally heated, it usually meant that there were heat registers cut in the floors to allow heat to move upstairs from a wood or coal-fired furnace.

Because countless new inventions changed the way business and home functioned, there was a deep and growing sense of possibility in the first decades of the twentieth century. Bicycles, cameras, and mail-order catalogs literally enlarged young peoples' worlds. Church played an important role in social differentiation, and one's membership in a particular congregation meant something about social position.

World War I and the 1918 Spanish Influenza epidemic killed large numbers of these young people and left the survivors more focused on the one hand, and more ready to play through the "Roaring Twenties" on the other. Relatively easy money and a growing economy while the oldest half (leading edge) of this cohort were marrying and beginning to raise children in the 1920's, were reflected in many of the handsome church buildings we see today. The availability of steel and concrete as relatively cheap building materials allowed construction of larger and more imposing structures than most congregations had been able to afford in earlier times.

This turned into hardship and fear in the 1930's. Churches struggled to survive, even though attendance was strong. The experience of the Great Depression changed the Builders' outlook from optimistic to realistic. Yet their experience of church as a socially stabilizing force did not diminish, and their training in top-down authority was reinforced by the growth of the government and the pervasiveness of the military model into the 1950's. Some of the oldest leading edge Builder men experienced World War I service, and many had older brothers or cousins who trained and fought. Nearly all participated in World War II in some capacity, as ordinary soldiers, sailors and marines and as officers, as well as in support functions and on "the home front."

Builders invested heavily in grand, beautiful church buildings and shrines, designed to honor God and those who inspired others. Ceremonies, parades and ritual reinforced their core values. Brass bands, organs and trumpets expressed their enthusiasm and determination.

They have experienced wave after wave of technological change throughout their lives, but writing and printing on paper has remained the most valued form of communication. In their retirement, their improved health and a greatly increased standard of living has allowed many of them to continue to play active roles in their communities and churches long after their own grandparents would have been gone. The youngest, now in their eighties and nineties, often have great-grandchildren, something their own grandparents' generation would not have experienced.

Silents—born 1924-1945

The leading-edge Silents' earliest memories were of the expansive years of the late Twenties, but all of them were hugely affected by the Great Depression and World War II, which in combination was their formative experience. By the time the eldest were into their teens, the shadow of World War was changing the shape of their world. The draft began in 1942 after the bombing of Pearl Harbor. Those men who were not drafted often enlisted, and everyone contributed to the war effort. If food had been scarce during the 1930's for many, it now became even harder to get. Milk, butter, sugar, eggs and meat were all shipped overseas to feed "our boys." Food, soap, cloth, leather goods and gasoline were rationed. Leg makeup was sold because silk and nylon (newly invented synthetic silk) were needed for parachutes.

This is a generation raised to "put up and shut up", to "save for a rainy day" and told to "use it up, wear it out; make it do, or do without." They were not asked their opinions, and were told "Children are better seen than heard." The adults simply had too many very serious issues to deal with, and children were to listen, behave and obey until they were old enough to help win the World War. Even when the war was over, it took years before there was enough housing and supplies to go around. Returning servicemen often had to return to their family's home to live. All they wanted to do after the War was marry, have a family and settle down in American liberty and security—in peace. But the Korean War and nuclear threat continued to remind them how fragile world peace was.

No wonder that the 1950's was a time deeply focused on family, church, raising children and secure employment. The military and industrial powerhouse that had helped win WWII now turned its attention to domestic products such as houses, appliances and automobiles. The officers moved into corporate jobs or their own businesses. Their wives ran volunteer organizations modeled on them. Ordinary soldiers and sailors moved into the blue-collar jobs that demanded their skills. Some started their own skilled labor companies. A single salary was considered enough in many homes, because demand for consumer goods was focused most heavily on basics. And they looked pretty good after years of restrictions. As the country's economy boomed, wages and salaries rose. And babies boomed, too. The largest cohort of children ever born in America began to make their appearance, and suddenly they were everywhere, demanding time, attention, and material goods.

The new sense of permissiveness in raising children in this safe world lasted into the 1960's and then exploded into something unexpected. The Silents were unprepared for the speed and the power of the change. The civil rights movement and the assassinations of the Kennedy brothers, Martin Luther King and others shook the very ground under their feet. Suddenly there was student unrest, psycho-active drugs, riots in major cities, and their own children singing Bob Dylan's song to them: "The Times They Are a'Changin." (As if they had not noticed!)

Churches became safe havens for sanity as they knew it. The church contained Truth. In the face of such eternal truth, one should be silent and reverential. The reassuring top-down authority, the respect and traditional language, and the ordered rows of families facing the altar and pulpit seemed like the elements of security in a world that was falling apart. Sitting in the same pew every week, seeing the same people, singing the same hymns has remained a valuable source of comfort for the Silents.

In the decades since the 1970's, they have mostly managed to maintain their congregational traditions, but are increasingly worried about the cost of maintenance and clergy. They worry that younger members will not have the resources or desire to keep their lovely buildings repaired or open. Many congregations have merged or closed. Church-attending Silents continue to see their congregations as places of identity, and deeply love and support the traditions there.

Silents moved fairly easily into senior positions in industry, church and other organizations. A very small cohort numerically, they have felt as though they finally achieved the positions they have earned by decades of hard work. Many have lived into their seventies and eighties in relatively good health, and many Silents now see no reason to retire or step down when their own life expectancies are ever longer. Yet most are also experiencing financial as well as medical restrictions. They know how to cope; they have been here before.

Boomers—born 1946-1960

It has only recently dawned on Boomers that the world has changed dramatically, and that it does not revolve around them. As Boomers are entering their fifties and sixties, they are horrified to discover that they really are getting older, and that GenXers are taking over as "the young." They took to cell phones like ducks to water, because the telephone is their formative technology. During their lifetimes they have moved from one or two phones per house to at least one cell phone per person. While many are adapting well to the newest electronic technology, others are acknowledging that it is moving too fast for them to keep up. And it is harder and harder to see those little screens and press those little keys—which keep getting larger in response.

Children of the Baby Boom were formed in a world that was deeply child-centered and family-grounded in the 1950's and '60's. They were raised in the top-down authority model of the churches and schools of their parents and grandparents and accepted it, just as they accepted the fact that the country would continue to get richer, and they would too. Boomers are a deeply material generation and are used to having the benefits of relatively cheap clothing, food and gasoline. They experience restriction as something to be put up with for a short time, until things "get back to normal." The recessions of the early 1970's and early 1980's were blips on their horizons. But once the Great Recession hit in 2008, they have found themselves in a world they do not understand, and getting poorer seems incomprehensible. They are slow to realize that their Boomer-Boom Times may not have been historically normal.

Boomers also have felt free to challenge, reject and desert many traditional institutions, including churches, during their lifetimes, secure in the belief that the old folks would keep them going, because that's what they always did. Yes, their war-protests had helped end the draft in 1973, but not before most of their cohort had either served in the military or known someone who was drafted. Yes, many had rejected corporate life for music and drugs, but the corporate jobs were still there when they needed money to buy a house and raise kids. Yes, many female Boomers had welcomed "the pill" and a career, but were a little horrified to discover that there was a biological limit to fertility. There are a lot of "last chance" babies among Boomer couples.

Boomers like their churches to look professional, their clergy to look professional, and their music to be highly produced. But they also want the freedom to write their own weddings and funerals. They were trained in school to be first with the answer, and want immediacy more than "rightness." Slow deliberation and silence appeal to relatively few Boomers. Some of the older and more traditionally minded Boomers have stepped into roles of congregational authority; but many others just leave until they want a marriage or funeral, or to celebrate Christmas and Easter. The churches have always been there, and presumably they always will. But now the Boomers are starting to wonder, as they are about a great many things: "What is normal?" "Will all the things I am used to still be there—my pension, my savings, my job and my house?"

Boomers are often confused and resentful of Gen Xers who still seem to have the youth that is mysteriously disappearing for them. They have a sense that they should be moving into the senior roles now, but Silents still seem to occupy a lot of them. And the GenXers seem to resent them in return, and lump them in with the remaining Builders and the many Silents as "old folks." Boomers? Old? Never!

GenX—born 1961/3—1981/4

GenX has very distinct leading edge and trailing edge characteristics, even though the calendar dates that mark the beginning and ending of this cohort are smudgy. The older group, a relatively small birth cohort (known to some as the Baby Bust), is now in their forties and early fifties. They have a foot in each half of the 'Older/Younger" generational divide that we will discuss at greater length in Chapter Three. They often play the role of translators and peacemakers between the generations because they understand both perspectives. They may also function more like Boomers in some situations and more like GenX in others.

As a whole, GenXers are rather cynical. They swallowed the Boomer idea of ever-increasing wealth and economic expansion, and it has not played out for them. They were raised by trailing edge Silents and leading edge Boomers for the most part, who really believed the world was getting better and they were causing it. GenXers were often latch-key children of dual income parents. They were dropped off for Sunday school or weeknight religious training. In their childhoods, they encountered professional child rearing experts, educational experts, psychological experts, environmental experts and had their recommended food groups changed every few years. They have been market targets since they were born, and nearly everything looks fake to them. Deeply affected by the economic problems of the late 1970's and early '80s, when many of their parents and parents' friends lost jobs, they learned that the way to succeed was to borrow. Since most Americans' incomes have been stagnant in real buying power since then, the explosive growth of the credit industry covered the shortfall.

During their early adult years in the 1980's and 1990's they experienced the failure of nearly everything that had made America "great"—the environment, the presidency, Challenger, American manufacturing, and stable families. Divorce rates have climbed steadily since they were born. Their world is global, and few still experience a homogeneous social world. They have been an increasingly integrated, multi-cultural, multi-gendered cohort since their childhood.

Born into the Age of Aquarius and New Age spiritual experimentation, GenXers are deeply interested in spirituality, but not in organized religion. Small groups, spontaneity and authentic relationships are far more attractive than large scheduled meetings. Electronic communication was invented for them, as it enabled their own "tribes" to stay intimately connected long after schooling and jobs had separated them. (A tribe is best defined as those with whom you are in daily electronic communication.)

Many are deeply resentful of the credit and mortgage scams they have suffered from, and of the Boomers and Silents they perceive as having foisted such burdens on them. The Great Recession has made economic anxiety real for them in a way that Silents understand and Boomers do not. They do not understand the Olders' world or why they are not being taken seriously as some are ready to step into senior leadership positions. This has encouraged many to start their own businesses, invent their own social structures, and separate themselves from the institutions and gatherings dear to the Olders' hearts. They do not see why they should invest time and energy in propping up things that seem outdated, rigid and controlled by Boomers and Silents who will not share authority.

On the other hand, some are finding smaller congregations which have lost most of their older members (and thus have leadership positions open) to be inviting and safe communities in which to raise their own crop of trailing edge Millennial and Gen Z babies. Ironically, the fact that many such congregations cannot afford full-time clergy may be fine with GenX. Since they themselves have so many competing demands for Sunday morning time, leading a service on Saturday or Sunday evening may work well for them. Priests and pastors who have other professional jobs are living the same kind of lives that their GenX peers are, and they may be very comfortable communicating with congregational leaders and members by electronic means. Others are forming their own separate worshiping communities, and these "emerging" churches often incorporate ancient church practices with little regard to mainline denominational traditions.

Millennials—born 1985-2001

Leading edge Millennials, now in their late teens and early twenties, are an electronically savvy, totally wired group that has both teenage e-entrepreneurs and back-at-home Peter Pans (never-grow-up, not me) being identified as characteristic of them. The truth is that nearly all are suffering badly from the employment meltdown of the Great Recession. Unlike their Boomer elders, they do not think that these are anomalies in the ever-upward trend of American greatness. They are more like GenXers in that regard. But they also are part of the new century of electronic invention, and do not think it is odd to have to replace their computers and electronic media devices every 18 months because they are obsolete.

Most Millennials have grown up in close communication with their parents by cell phone and texting. Helicopter parents (hovering, hovering) have scheduled their non-school hours with activities, and they suffer from acceptance of their underachievement in the name of non-harm. Used to a constant stream of appreciation, many are having trouble moving into the work world of the 21st century with its intense focus on value-producing labor. They may have spent little unstructured face-to-face time during their school years and many have difficulty in knowing how to handle it. Instead, they retreat to the electronic world of social networks and games. Face-to-face gatherings may involve every person physically present playing the same electronic game, rather than direct personal interaction.

Millennials at the same time are idealistic and sure that their generation will solve many of the environmental, medical and social issues that confront the country. Of any cohort, they tend to be the least concerned about race, gender, or cultural issues. They like well designed clothing, equipment and electronics. Trailing edge Millennial girls wear their mismatched socks, leggings, boots and fancy dresses to church with pride and are supported by their parents, who like their "funky" look. Millennial boys are exhibiting more and more anger and frustration as they are channeled into supervised sports and violent electronic games rather than the physical rough and tumble games of their Olders.

Millennials also understand that they will have multiple employment/ self-employment roles over the course of their lives. They have experienced stay-at-home parents who work electronically as well as parents who have had to learn new jobs and new skills in a challenging economy. Many fewer anticipate owning a permanent house, but expect to move throughout their lives as new employment or business opportunities open up. Many Millennials already function in real and virtual dollar-producing activities in the electronic world. They do not expect to live in a single community with stable neighbors, and many have foreclosed houses in their neighborhoods. But their electronic networked world offers them other forms of social connection with family, friends and peers. Millennials do not find *The Church of Facebook* to be an odd title for a printed book. (See bibliography.)

Most are too young to have strong congregational presence, but they do like to participate in church service projects and music when their parents take them. Leading edge Millennials have begun to make commitments to faith communities, but they are equally likely to create their own spiritual gatherings. Sacred arts, with their strong aesthetic appeal, may well attract them. Their cohort's years came to an abrupt end on September 11, 2001.

GenZ—born 2001-2020?

While our GenZers are still too young to say much about themselves, we can heave a sigh of relief that they are still children—seemingly the only remaining recognizable element of the old three-generation model. This is true until their parents and grandparents discover that they have been texting an "older friend" for three months. God bless us all!

Questions:

1) Ask yourself again, which cohort do I resonate with? How about my parents? My children, students, nieces or nephews?

2) Do I know people in other cohorts? Do I know them very well?

3) Which cohorts are represented in my immediate neighborhood?

4) Which cohort(s) are our clergy in? Which cohorts do our key congregational leaders belong to? Has my perception changed after reading the cohort descriptions?

5) If our congregation has multiple worship services, which cohorts attend each?

6) Are certain ministries or programs filled with only one or two cohorts?

   Which, if any, are multigenerational?

Chapter Three

The Generational Divide

Too many generational cohorts have been trying to compact themselves into three social roles in America for the last three decades. So now it may be clearer that the three-generation normative model of leader elders, worker bees in the middle raising kids, and the children themselves, has survived long past its universal historical presence. Yet it is still the default model for organization in multi-generational settings with widely spaced aged groupings. As an example, look at nursery school children visiting a Seniors' center, organized by the teachers. Teenagers interviewing older neighborhood residents for an oral history project organized by community leaders might be another example. It would be very unusual for a group of GenXers to interview Boomers about what their youth was like, even though the oldest and youngest of them might be separated by 35 years.

Today so many adults and those functioning as adults are crowding the stage that social situations are getting more challenging to negotiate. In our congregations, leaders are noticing something odd: unless there is a strong multigenerational presence, often functioning in a single multipurpose worship and fellowship space, either the Boomers or the GenXers may have "won." Either one group or the other may be present, but not usually both in significant numbers, unless the congregation is very small, very well integrated in its power structures, or large enough to have separate niches for each group.

What is at work is the generational divide we examined briefly in Chapter One, and now will look at again in greater detail. In the next pages, by painting this issue with a very broad brush, we will explore the issues that separate Gen Xers and Boomers. But first a few warnings.

There are large regional differences in congregations' experience of these issues. Small local congregations with strong multigenerational family bonds may not find these challenges relevant. Southern and/ or conservative congregations may have well-developed formation practices that work in their environments to integrate generational cohorts. Western and northwestern non-urban congregations may be so small that generational interests are secondary to their concerns. Ethnic congregations may use their cultural heritage to help negotiate power issues by role-definitions that apply to gender and/or age distinctions.

Nevertheless, in most American states, there are six generational cohorts alive and well. And congregations may have some or all of them represented in their membership. In many congregations, the biggest generational tension seems to be between the Boomers and the GenXers. Why should this be?

As we mentioned in Chapter One, there are essential differences in worldview between these two cohorts. It is worthwhile restating them because we can best understand the generational divide through the lenses of worldview and technological change.

1) Those who are now over the age of fifty were raised by people who had experienced the personal and societal discipline of global war. Their parents and grandparents had lived through the realities and horrors of World War I. Only 25 years later, all the young men were drafted into World War II. Food, clothing and gasoline were rationed at home. The at-home population understood and abided by the top-down discipline required to win the war, because the lives of thousands of American males between the ages of 18 and 40 literally depended upon it.

2) The change in technology between 1950 and 2010 is almost hard to describe. A person who reached adulthood before 1975 and a person who reached adulthood after 1985 essentially live in different worlds. Our GenXers and those who are younger live in a world that is much flatter, without much of the top-down authority that was so needed in the World Wars. They have never experienced whole-population discipline or the draft, but they have global communication. They have never experienced food rationing, but they have much better understanding of global

demand for oil and the ping-pong curves of the international market. GenXers have a deep understanding of an electronic world that it is organized by skill and will and market share, but not by age-hierarchy.

What is the generational divide? To summarize (and perhaps to over-generalize), it will be helpful to say that the Olders were formed in an age-graded society with top-down authority, and the Youngers function in a flatter, team-based society based on skills and payments for service that are available 24/7 through electronic media. Another way (once again overstated) to highlight the generational divide is to note that Olders' worldview is based on earned and chronological credentials, and consists of a sequential pathway through which you work and age. Youngers function in a world with separately segmented understandings of life: "act this way in this location; act another way in that." At the same time, in ways that mystify Olders, for many Youngers all of life is tied together by an increasingly seamless electronic network.

The Olders understand the three-generation model with its foundational concept of age and rank as authority sources because the world seemed to function that way when they were young and being formed. Builders and Silents raised their children (the Boomers) in this model. The Youngers' experience a six-cohort society with children, young people transitioning into the workforce (while interspersed with training periods), two middle-stage adult segments, retired active elders, and the feeble Old. Most of these are linked (or should be!) by a variety of electronic media and communication technology, in which paid professionals offer highly specialized services (lawyers, doctors, architects, clergy, e.g.) and have "authority" in their own area. Such professionals do not have much social authority. It is not clear where such social authority resides in the world as they see it.

How does this play out in our congregations?

The Boomers and their elders were formed in congregations that look back to a history of age-graded authority. In the broad catholic traditions, senior males hold the power in a well articulated series of hierarchical, named positions. Exceptional females might develop personal authority across the church by their own skills and influence, but their recognized power came at the top of parallel female organizations.

At the local congregational level, these traditionally occurred within the dominant male structure. (Think of parochial schools, traditionally taught by female religious sisters who answered to the pastor, as well as to their own religious orders, and of Protestant Women's Committees subject to all-male Boards and clergy.)

The Protestant Reformation did not materially change male power structures. While different denominations accepted female preachers and ministers at different times after the Reformation, most did not make provision for the regular ordination of women into primary congregational leadership roles until the last half of the 20th century. The Quakers are a notable exception in this regard; some conservative evangelical denominations still do not ordain women to primary authority roles.

Thus, most fifty-and-older Americans had a formative experience of religion that emphasized a senior male Pastor with a (mostly) senior male congregational Board.

Another important characteristic of the formational communities we call congregations, is that community worship is traditionally seen as the primary work of the church. People "went to church" on Sunday because the gathering of the community was important in and of itself. One participated in that community in age and gender appropriate ways. Different denominations sorted out roles and responsibilities differently: the elders did the primary worship; the worker-bees ran the church school and hospitality efforts, served on committees and in ancillary roles; and the children did what they were told and taught. Attendance was noted. Advancement was strictly by age for children, and by achievement and regular participation by worker bees. Eventually their faithfulness was rewarded by election or selection for congregational leadership posts. For women it might be head of the Sunday School or President of the Women's Group; for men, it was being head of a Committee. After many years there was tacit promotion into the leadership generation as a reward for faithful service and membership.

Worship was attended by a congregation who sat looking at the backs of each others' heads, and facing the senior Pastor and assisting ministers. (This is still the case in most American churches today.) This was consistent with the troops facing the commanding officer, or the seated employees facing management. Advancement was also by achievement and regular attendance in the military and corporate worlds. Women's groups organized themselves in parallel systems.

Recognition of promotion through these age-graded systems included titles, medals, permission to enjoy certain privileges, and in the congregation, access to certain religious rituals and sacraments. Credentials were an essential part of this system, and the issuance of credentials by a duly constituted authority was essential to its maintenance. The credentialed person was both licensed and authorized to act in a social role, and carried the weight of authority in (usually) himself. Everyone knew the system and powerful social norms reinforced it. Liturgy followed authorized denominational guidelines, set by denominational leaders. Church music came from an approved source, often a printed hymnal or sacred music canon. There was a deep expectation that whatever one experienced, it had been approved at the top, was carried out by those licensed or appointed to do it, and was to be learned and mastered by children and youth.

The church was an attractive employer for many young men before 1965, because it offered secure advancement through denominational levels of seniority and the added cachet of social authority. The clergy were among the most educated and admired of the traditional leaders of the community. They were accorded a very high degree of respect. Elected male congregational leaders were generally admired. Church Board Presidents/Wardens achieved the same local social dignity over the years that Mayors and School Superintendents achieved.

The country had survived two World Wars and the Great Depression by maintaining discipline and building capacity. Saving money, tradition, respect for authority and following the rules marked most congregational life. The model was clear: elders governed, younger adults worked and raised children, and children obeyed (or learned how to appear as though they were doing so.) Only those who experienced an old fashioned one or two-room schoolhouse escaped some of the pressures of the inexorable K-12 system.

Those who did not wish to participate in this world did so very quietly. Staying home on Sunday morning to read the newspaper was not admired, but since most stores honored "blue laws" that kept them closed on Sunday, there was not much else to do. Before 1965, Sunday morning was reserved for communities gathering in worship congregations, church and family activities, and little else.

GenXers and those younger

By 1980, when the first GenXers were teenagers, the world they experienced was profoundly different than it had been for Boomers in the 1950's and early '60's. The thirty-some years between then and today has made age-graded, top-down, male-dominated authority far less common. Only in our schools does the age-graded experience survive, and it is giving way to skill-based and team learning, or home schooling that emphasizes skill acquisition over chronological age segregation. Many high schools offer submatriculation into community colleges or technical schools. In the military services, and Catholic and Orthodox churches the male-dominated authority structure does survive, but it is under at least some assault.

Beginning with GenX, most children are now raised in homes where mid-20th century gender roles have been modified to a greater or lesser degree to reflect the realities of dual-income schedules or the harder single parent role. Many GenXers experienced being "latch-key" children as both parents went out to work. Traditional marriages are continuing to decline, with more adults opting to raise children without a spouse. The 2010 Census confirms that as many as half of households with children have unmarried parents. A child's father(s) often play a very different role than GenXers' own fathers and grandfathers did. Household structure, as we have noted, varies greatly. Many single fathers and adoptive fathers under fifty are raising children.

Those under forty function in a skill-based world where they often fill multiple roles at different authority levels. They may be a Vice President in one setting, and a beginner somewhere else, while they also hone active skills in a third area of expertise—often athletic or avocational. The marathon runner may also write a regular, widely read blog, and be part of a virtual planning team in the business world. A stay-at-home parent may work with data from another country every evening and make money selling custom birthday cakes to a local bakery. This multiple identity lifestyle is united by a seamless 24/7 electronic network. Leadership is *ad hoc* and situational in most settings. GenXers' children do not automatically assume that a male is the one "in charge."

Congregations traditionally do not create leadership roles for many below age 40, and the church itself is not seen as an attractive career option for most Youngers. A clergy career no longer offers the promise of social authority or role-deference it did fifty years ago. Instead for many younger people, the church may be seen as a provider of spiritual services as a caterer is a provider of food. Both are available on a pay-per-event basis for weddings and funerals. Clergy in this model are paid professionals with certain skills, available as are other paid professionals. It is hard for clergy to comprehend—if they have been formed into the old three-generational model—that their authority is perceived to lie in the function of what they do, rather than the named position they occupy. They may have the authority to perform a wedding or a funeral in the church, but are expected to have little to say about the rest of the wedding weekend or funeral reception, which is a purely secular affair. And they are not necessarily assumed to have broad social insights or authority. (There are ethnic and cultural exceptions to this.)

Younger people may have had Sunday-school-only experience of church and congregational life, and their departure from congregations after their mid-teens has now become the norm. Increasingly, they and their younger peers are being raised to know *how* to attend church in the same way that their parents teach them *how* to go to a restaurant. The congregation rarely functions any longer as a community organizing structure. Parents may travel long distances to bring their children to "Mom-mom's" church once a month, Christmas and Easter, but maintain relatively fragile connections with that congregation themselves.

In her insightful book, *Tribal Church*, Carol Howard Merritt, a young Presbyterian minister, describes the difference that GenXers and Millennials experience in trying to attend a traditional church. It simply does not work in terms of the realities of their own lives.

She uses the concept of *tribe*, which is essential to understand for those 50 and older, if this Younger worldview is to make any sense to them. It is a product of instantaneous electronic communication and the nearly universal use of it by those under 40. For purposes of this discussion, we'll define *tribe* as: those with whom one is in (almost) daily personal electronic communication. For kids, this may be their families and classmates. For teens and older, it will almost always include far distant friends, family and business associates, web-friends and web-associates (such as media contacts, bloggers, or those who regularly schedule podcasts.) It may also include web-avatars of those persons and sources.

This means that in any face-to-face gathering (church, event, meeting, or classroom), those physically present will represent their tribe and they may be in continuous contact with them during the face-to-face time. Those physically present may also be in electronic communication with others physically present. It is not unusual for a group of younger people to text others who are physically present in the same room, even while they are pursuing their individual interests on their laptop screens or electronic text device. This baffles Olders.

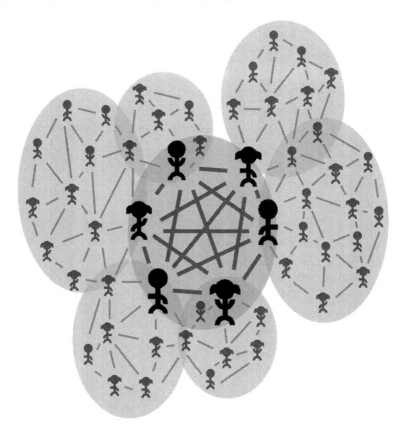

In the old face-to-face world, only those physically present (those in the middle oval) were involved directly (indicated by heavy lines) in a meeting or event. In the tribal world, each person physically present will also bring other members of their tribe (represented in the surrounding networks) into the room electronically. It is wise to ask: "Who else is here with us?"

If there is a single complaint of Olders about Youngers, it is over the 24/7 electronic network that links them to each other. Olders want this turned off in face-to-face gatherings. Youngers are confused and horrified at the idea of being cut off from their identity source, their families and their friends for even a short while.

This non-privileging of face-to-face interaction means that younger people are mystified by the constant long, often non-productive meetings that characterize traditional three-generation church, where the gathering itself reinforces community and hierarchy. Their nearly universal electronic access to information also leads younger people to question the value of top-down educational practices connected with many traditional Sunday school and Christian formation programs. Their own learning process is far more experiential than philosophical, and they are impatient with material that assumes a certain age-progression or requires memorization.

The music wars in congregations are legendary. Why depend on a Hymnal when you can download anything? What's the point of sitting looking at the back of someone's head when you interact with your music online or watch videos?

Today, Sunday mornings are packed with sports and the gym, coffeehouse and family conversations, laptop interactions and charity or service opportunities, as well as regularly scheduled work for many employees. Congregations offer few of these, and for forty-and-youngers attendance once a month is a sign of active membership. Social networks and tribes are making face-to-face gatherings that expect the whole household to appear together and fit into age-graded, top-down social structures a rare event.

The often repeated explanation: *I'm spiritual but not religious* reflects these folks' sincere desire for a relationship with God or the spiritual world that is unmediated by denominational structures or social strictures. They have immediate access to music, worship services, blogs and videos about spirituality. Why drag the whole exhausted household to church every Sunday? No wonder many congregational leaders are discovering that Youngers will show up for a one-time event but are extremely hard to pin down for volunteer service or regularly scheduled meetings.

What the Olders fail to see and value are the structures of social networks, tribes and electronic protocols that do integrate the Youngers. They are nearly invisible to them, and the Olders do not understand why they should be privileged above face-to-face, the highest reward situation for most traditional Olders. What the Youngers see instead is disrespect for their achievements, an insistence on a single-stream communication mode, and a weird refusal to participate in the electronic, networked society they inhabit.

No wonder clergy find themselves constantly translating between and among cohorts. Some clergy have even described their ability to "code switch" as being bilingual. No wonder clergy and congregational leaders struggle to understand their own congregations! When the Olders are pleased, the Youngers are absent. Yet when the Youngers are pleased, the Olders may be angry.

The blessing of our 40-50 year-olds: the Transition Decade

If these descriptions of the generational divide seem overdrawn to you, you may be among those born between 1960 and 1970, or have a congregation with a significant number of the transition decade in attendance. These are people with a foot in each camp. Especially if they have older siblings, they understand the fifty-plus worldview. However, it is likely that at work they function in the forty-and-unders' global, 24/7 electronic world. Many delayed child-bearing and –rearing until their thirties (1990-2000); many have second marriages or later household formation with adopted or step-children. And they are the peacemakers who understand the importance of written communications for olders and electronic media for youngers. They are "fluent" in both modes.

They are often called upon to act as translators and bridges. If your congregation is lucky enough to have one of these people as clergy, or a significant number on the church board, the perils and challenges of the generational divide will be greatly eased. If you have none, please see the reading list!

Questions:

1) If you are an Older, what insights about your own congregation have you had as you read this chapter? If you are a Younger, what insights have you had?

2) Does your congregation have any 40-50 year old "peacemakers" or translators?

3) What do Olders need to learn from Youngers?

4) What do Youngers need to learn from Olders?

Suggested Reading—See the Bibliography for full information

Generational Issues in the Church

Tribal Church, Carol Howard Merritt

The Church of All Ages, Howard Vanderwell

Reaching People under 40 while Keeping People over 60, Edward Hammett with James R. Pierce (Find a good discussion of the first five cohorts in Chapter 3: "When Generations Collide")

The Church of Facebook: How the Hyperconnected Are Redefining Community, Jesse Rice

Generational Relationships in the Business World

Generations at Work: Managing the Clash of Veterans, Boomers, Xers and Nexters in Your Workplace, Ron Zemke, Claire Raines, Bob Filipczak

Millennials Incorporated: The Big Business of Recruiting, Managing and Retaining the World's New Generation of Young Professionals, Lisa Orrell

Chapter Four

Realities for Congregational Life

How should congregational leaders function in a six-cohort society? Relax! No one is quite sure yet.

Here's what we do know. The old model of three generations which has served the church well for centuries no longer describes the society in which we find ourselves. The new reality is that six generational cohorts are struggling to find appropriate roles in a society less and less defined by chronological age. The oldest half of the Builders cohort is no longer playing active adult roles, but many spry and wise 90 year olds are very active. The GenZers are clearly still children. But as much as half the Builders' cohort, many of the Silents, the Boomers, GenXers and Millennials are increasingly crowding the two classic adult roles of Elder/Leader and Worker Bees. Their ages range from 15 to 90. In the Three Generation Society face-to-face world, age and credentials mattered a great deal. In the Six Generation society that functions through the electronic world, chronological age has little relevance, for that world is based on performance, skills and connections far more than on physical age.

If it were a matter of simply replacing one model with another, the issue would be as sharply highlighted as it is in an Anthony Trollope or Edith Wharton novel. But it is not that simple. While it is being replaced by a flatter, networked, team-based paradigm in some parts of our society, the Three Generation model continues to shape basic household and social face-to-face interactions. There are the usual tensions between elders and middles, and between middles and youngers. The 70 year old caring for a 95 year old is just older and wearier than the 50 year old caring for a 75 year old. The classic conflicts of parents raising children have not changed, even though child-rearing patterns have changed dramatically. A 2010 Pew Research Center Report, *Millennials: Confident. Connected. Open to Change*, noted that older Millennials are the most likely to have parents who are divorced or unmarried. Teenagers are still teenagers, but now young adults join them in transitional roles. The comic strip "Dustin" explores what it means for a family to have working parents, kids going to school, and a 20-something who stays home.

What the six-cohort society does is add another layer of complexity to the old tensions and conflicts. What about that 26 year old still living at home, only partially employed and staying up till 3 am every night, while his 50 year old parents get up at 6 and go to work, leaving him perhaps with his 96 year old great-grandparent who needs daycare services? What about the 38 year old single parent whose daughter just had a baby with her boyfriend and expects help, and whose own 61 year old mother is still working and needs help in turn with her ill 86 year old parent?

All six generational cohorts rarely physically inhabit the same space at the same time. Business is dealing with some of these issues, and a few helpful books are trying to explore the workplace challenge of integrating Silents, Boomers, GenXers and Millennials into productive teams. (References to them appear at the end of the last chapter.) A temporary social solution has been segregation and niche services. Restaurants and bars tend to separate the texters and non-texters by appealing to different markets. Multiple generations do inhabit the same Internet, and the horror of discovering one's grandparents on Facebook is legendary. On her talk show, Tyra warns those under 18 never to make sexual contacts on the Internet. Until recently, Oprah dealt with the Boomer set's issues.

Yet all six generations may, however briefly, inhabit the same congregation. In fact, churches and synagogues are one of the few places where all six cohorts may come together and interact authentically. Baptisms, Bar/Bat Mitzvahs, weddings and funerals, as well as the most sacred holy days, invite and expect everyone. That's when the generational divide may add yet another layer of conflict through worldview and technology mismatches.

In Chapters One through Three, we have sketched out the demographic and sociological issues that are making the old three-generation paradigm less and less useful for clergy and lay leaders who are struggling to make sense of what they encounter. As we have noted, Olders are deeply frustrated at the active or passive refusal of the Youngers to participate deeply in traditional church structures (all puns intended). There is frustration for GenX and older Millennials as well, especially those raising children. On the one hand (three generational model), they seem to fit in well, as the church traditionally has done a fine job of supporting parents raising young children; but on the other hand (the six generation reality), GenXers have a constant sense that they are falling short of some voiced—and many more unvoiced—expectations.

The positive expectations for GenXers go something like this: *We want you to participate in our congregation, raise your children in faith, and find loving support here, **the same way we did.*** The unvoiced negative expectations would sound more like this: *We can't believe that you are allowing your children to text during worship and Sunday School, that you only show up once a month or so, and that you seem so unwilling to participate in all the work that binds our congregation together and keeps our buildings in good repair. **We wouldn't do that.*** On the other hand, the GenXers' own interior monologue is saying: *You don't seem to respect the difficult choices I am making about raising my children in a dangerous, expensive world where I cannot control their access to internet predators, bullying, school violence and drugs. **Why don't you get it?***

The challenge and the opportunities for congregations are enormous. If we hope to continue our congregational lives in a six generational cohort society, church leaders must become deeply aware of all the generational issues: three, six and the generational divide. And yes, it is complex and confusing!

By now, you may well have some insights about how this three-generational-model-six-cohort reality is playing out in your congregation, or the one down the street. Let's explore some examples of how the multiple layers of generational friction are at work in some of today's congregations in the following Congregational Moment. As you read, ask yourself whether you identify with any of the people in the story, and where your own sympathies lie. Then try reading it again from another character's perspective, and see if your perceptions change.

A Congregational Moment

Kaitlyn was running late that afternoon. She raced out of work at 4 and still had not prepared for the Team meeting the next morning. After grabbing her laptop, she texted her 10-year-old to meet her on the corner outside school in 20 minutes. On the way, she pulled into the convenience store, grabbed five deli sandwiches and a bag of baby carrots. When she collected Ben, they talked about his day and his pleasure at landing the part in the annual Church play that he wanted so badly. He'd had a walk-on role last year, and was stage-struck. She was pleased, because she'd felt the same way as a kid, and still loved children's theater.

She rolled in, deposited the food on the kitchen counter and sent him upstairs to do his homework. Kaitlyn put the basket of underwear and socks she had sorted that morning into the washer, and folded the towels in the dryer. She put notes for her two older children on the refrigerator so they'd know what to eat after their sports practice, and said to be sure to leave one sandwich for their father, who would be in late. Calling Ben for dinner at 6, she unwrapped two sandwiches and put some of the carrots in a bowl with yogurt dip. Ben was late, she was hungry. He played with his sandwich, and she suspected he'd been eating candy from his backpack upstairs. At 6:30 they left for church. She brought her laptop. At least she'd be able to sit and work while he rehearsed.

No sooner had she settled into a chair in the shabby church hall, when in walked two 50-something women, Marilyn and Sue, that she had met after worship a couple of months ago. When they greeted her and sat down on the couch nearby, she groaned inwardly. As it turned out, they wanted her to become the co-chair of the Christmas cookie exchange this year. They explained that it had been started by the oldest member of the congregation, and the tradition was now in its 47th year. Kate tried to explain that she was too busy, and did not know any of the recipes. No problem! The older women would be happy to share the recipes, and all Kate would have to do was find a dozen or so cooks. "We've all done our part over the years" they said, "and you know so many of the younger women. It's your turn now." Kate mentally groaned again, not even imagining that she'd find two who could spare the time for this, and thought how much of her own time she'd have to sacrifice in organizing it. "Perhaps we could buy them?" she asked.

Marilyn and Sue looked at each other in dismay, and explained that making and decorating the cookies together was part of the fun. Kate muttered that she would think about it and get back to them. Clutching her laptop, she went out to sit in the car and finish her work.

At 8:30 she found Ben and headed home. She again sent him upstairs to do his homework. She checked on the other two, and remembered the socks. Damn! She'd forgotten to put the socks in the dryer, and she still had not checked her personal e-mails. Her husband phoned to say he'd been delayed, and would be in about 10 pm, as the interviews had gone well but continued longer than planned.

The phone rang. It was Larry, the Church Council president, who had just turned 68. His birthday party had been held at church last weekend, she knew. Larry wanted to talk with her about serving on the Church Council next year. 'We are willing to have some younger people on the Council, and you have become very involved in our life together. We all think very highly of you, and think you will be a fine member, despite only having worshiped with us for a year or two. Sue and Marilyn tell me that they have asked you to be co-chair of the Cookie Exchange, and I know Ben is one of the stars of this year's Play. We don't see your husband and other two children as much as we would like, but perhaps if you are a member of Council, they will participate more in our church family. We'd also expect you to serve on one of the major Committees as part of your Council responsibilities."

Kate looked at the phone as though it might be a snake that had offered to bite her. "Uh, I don't think I can do that, Larry. My life's pretty busy right now. And in fact, I need to say good-bye because I still have laundry to do tonight if my family is going to have clean clothes tomorrow." She could hear the affront in his voice as he stiffly said good night. The socks! The dryer! Right.

Later, when Larry and Marilyn discussed Kate's refusing the honor of a Council position at such a young age, they agreed that the younger generation just did not want to work and was not very sociable. But they wondered who would take up the responsibilities when they could no longer handle them.

What is going on in this Congregational Moment is more than an old-fashioned clash between generational styles, and it has wider implications than may be apparent on the surface. While older members always want to recruit newer younger members to continue ministries, events and governance, this time there are two cohorts trying to recruit a younger one. Larry, a Silent, is more focused on Kaitlyn's youth as an exception to his expected practice of electing elders. Marilyn and Sue, Boomers, are more focused on handing over the work to younger people. They have "done their part through the years."

Marilyn and Sue are mystified that anyone could think that you can buy the cookies that are a part of a tradition of home baking, decorating and sharing. They wonder whether Kaitlyn had a mother who could not or did not cook. Perhaps she was brought up differently than they had raised their children. But she had seemed so normal.

Larry is hurt. He had put Kaitlyn's name forward as a candidate for Council, and even though she has only been attending for a year or two, he thought she would be flattered by this invitation and could scarcely refuse such an honor. He was completely unprepared for her apparently off-hand refusal and disinterest. Being cut short so that she could do laundry—and at that hour—makes him feel undervalued and disrespected. He has spent years faithfully serving the church, and he resents her not giving him more time and at least the courtesy of a longer conversation.

Kaitlyn is aware that Marilyn, Sue and Larry are all disappointed with her, but cannot take on one more thing. If she did, it would probably involve an hour at a spa once a week or going out for a drink with her friends. She can't imagine sitting around at endless church meetings or spending any more time than she already does at church. Kaitlyn herself is feeling resentful. Don't these old folks know how tired she is, and how much effort it takes to bring Ben to the rehearsals? If she did not want her son to enjoy the things she had enjoyed, and to know how to go to church, she would much rather get caught up on sleep Sunday mornings. Their father has supported the older two in their refusal to attend church very often, but Ben's interest in the play has given him a different perspective. Don't they see that?

The Challenge for Congregational Leaders

Kaitlyn lives in, and is raising her Millennials in, a world that operates very differently than Larry's, Marilyn's or Sue's. Because the worldview and technology issues we discussed in Chapter Three make the generational divide more intensely experienced by players on each side, emotional outcomes are exacerbated. Should Larry, Marilyn, Sue and Kaitlyn decide to discuss their feelings with their Pastor, they might or might not find understanding and good counsel.

Clergy may feel attacked on every side by upset people. Generational discussions nearly always bring heavy emotional loads with them, and far too often, the emotional baggage that generational and worldview clashes produce becomes targeted at clergy and parish leaders. Clergy have no more training in six generational reality than anyone else in our society! In fact, they may be deeply hampered by seminary training that took the three generation model as a given, and has done little if anything to prepare them for generational divide issues.

There is often little opportunity for discussion before accusations begin, and clergy may easily take such accusations at face value. When issues are complex and new, older sets of expectations are commonly used to evaluate what is happening. It is hard not to take such accusations personally. But if the church is to emerge from the six-generational cohort experience as a stronger and more faithful body, it will be essential to help congregants learn to look at the three primary factors we have been discussing in every clash between age groups: 1) the outmoded three-generation model; 2) technology, and 3) shift in worldview.

The challenge for congregational leaders will be to communicate not only what is happening, but our collective need to find a way forward that provides adequate comfort and support for each cohort. Often a conversational opening comes from the oldest members who are experiencing a deep sense of loss and confusion, and who reach out to clergy and congregational leaders to express their pain.

Teaching the new reality to Olders and Youngers may not be easy. Let's look at another Congregational Moment. Again, as you read, ask yourself whether you identify with any of the people in the story, and where your own sympathies lie. Try to assign each of the players a cohort identity as well as a religious perspective.

A Congregational Moment

The voice on the other end of the phone was older and very upset. "It's Audrey. I'm calling you because you understand our church. And you are old enough to understand what I am going to say. I'm so horrified, I can't believe my eyes. Do you know what is printed in our Newsletter? Did you see the invitation to this event for young people?"

The Assistant Pastor didn't know what had upset Audrey, but the Newsletter was in a stack on the table and he fished it out as he asked her for more details. "It's called *Bible and Brew*" she said, her voice nearly breaking with tears. "The seminarian is doing it. She must be learning some very strange things in Seminary these days. And I can't believe that our Senior Pastor did not put a stop to it. What was the Church Board thinking, to allow such a thing? And to encourage young people to drink, in the name of religion! What have we come to, if they can put the Bible and beer together? I want to get several of the older members together after church on Sunday to talk about this. We must think about how to give better guidance to our seminarians. Is it just because she is so young? What has happened to my church?"

Audrey is in her eighties, and has been a member for many years. The second-career Assistant Pastor could well understand why she was distressed. At the same time, he knew the GenXers in the congregation were excited about the upcoming event. As he replied to Audrey, he felt as though he was translating from a different language. He struggled to explain to her that many churches are now moving out into the community to find those under forty in the places where they are comfortable, rather than waiting until they come into our churches. *Bible and Brew* should be understood as a way to meet with young folks for discussion and evangelism that reflects the world in which they live. "If our clergy want to engage younger adults in conversations about their religious beliefs and lives, they will need to be willing to go to them," he said.

As they spoke, Audrey acknowledged that she had not seen many 20 or 30 year-olds in church recently, and that there were a great many grey and silver heads at the main worship service. He reminded her that Jesus himself had gone out to the people, to find them where they lived and worked, and had eaten and drunk with them at their tables.

"But what will become of our churches, if we go out to them, and they don't want to come to us?" she asked. He really had no answer, but to tell her that things always change, and perhaps the church must, too.

Audrey has every reason to be upset. There is simply no room in her understanding of deference, respect and church for putting alcohol and Scripture together, even on paper. When she was young in Prohibition times, beer was not legal anywhere in the country. When she was a young adult, many of the restrictions on drinking, religious and social, were still in place. No respectable clergyman would be seen in a tavern or bar in the 1940's, '50's and '60's. Even in the '70's and '80's, most would have felt out of place, and would certainly not have visited such places dressed in clerical clothing. Today, many clergy of conservative denominations would still find it unacceptable to drink (if they do at all) in public.

GenX targets of evangelism probably do not share this same reluctance, have probably not heard much about Prohibition or what caused it, and are far more likely to be able to tell you about their favorite micro-brew than name the minor prophets in the Bible.

Such changes in worldview are leaving many congregations struggling to understand what is happening. Whether or not American families ever matched the three-generation model is irrelevant to the power of the model to explain expected behavior to the Olders. Whether or not Youngers ever experienced a rigidly age-graded environment except in school, they also are struggling with the first six-cohort society the planet has ever known. As we said earlier, this is a complex and multilayered problem: the model is three; the reality is six and the generational divide makes substantive communication very difficult.

And because the three-generation church is iconic, some of the conversations that might happen among adults between the ages of 25 to 85 fail to occur for an odd reason. If three generational cohorts are present—say Silents, GenXers and Millennials, or older Boomers, younger GenXers and GenZers—there are representatives of three generations present, and that satisfies the model. Unless you have become sensitized to the six cohorts, a gathering with three cohorts will feel "right" and complete. When you understand the six cohort concept, you will immediately note who is present and who is missing.

Audrey inhabits a three-generation world of Builders, Silents and Boomers, which seems quite normal to her. She occasionally sees someone's great-grandchild, but does not interact with Youngers on a regular basis. Audrey is not realizing that she is looking across four generational cohorts when she sees a 25 year old. Youngers associate mostly with Youngers, and lump Olders into a single category—much to the Boomers' distress. It takes training and a perceptual effort to identify which cohorts are participating in any given event.

Community gatherings of all six cohorts are rare and can feel very awkward if appropriate roles have not been assigned to the participants. Given the Olders' privileging of regularly scheduled face-to-face meetings and the Youngers' lack of tolerance for repetitive gatherings, opportunities for genuine sharing across the generational divide are unusual. Sharing is more likely to occur within generational cohorts than between them. The generational divide between the Boomers and GenXers is, as we have discussed, the most acute.

Small congregations often work out these challenges in family-like ways, idiosyncratically and locally, if they remain vital and strong. Large congregations can afford multiple worship, outreach/service and program options to serve each cohort segment. The middle-size congregation often has a missing cohort or two, as that eases the tensions.

Some congregations, regardless of size, just hunker down, waiting for all this to pass. It is not only Olders who may refuse to budge. Some younger Boomers and even some older GenXers who were raised in the old model are determined to hold onto it, and are working tirelessly to raise their own children in the three-generational model. Recently a 48-year-old mother of three (a self-acknowledged trailing-edge Boomer) said she was just waiting until her children grew up and could take over from the GenXers who have critical mass in her congregation. She explained that she does not permit her children to text, makes them attend worship together as a family, and expects them to "take back the church" as soon as they get old enough. "I'll hang on until they do!" she promised.

These stresses are felt by clergy, too. Older clergy may not have to or want to deal with the missing Youngers. Many Older clergy are mostly unaware that there is a problem. They may try to rest in an authority that is increasingly fragile. They may also wonder why "the younger generation" seems to be getting so conservative, not realizing that only Youngers who like and are seeking traditionalist congregations are attracted to their church.

Younger clergy, now mostly GenXers and a few of the oldest Millennials, are finding that they are often acting as translators for their congregations, and that the Olders seem not to hear their voices. They wonder why their Olders often counsel them to "Act like a real leader! Share your plan and vision for this church!" in a top-down, not team-based style that is foreign to them. In larger churches, they fear becoming niche-pastors, serving only their own cohorts, and losing touch with the Olders in the congregation. Yet many are glad to find themselves in Assistants' roles (with Boomer or Silent senior pastors who can address Olders' concerns). Both Older and Younger clergy may be comfortable as leaders of more conservative or ethnic congregations that are held together by shared beliefs that define them as separate from the secular world, rather than to try leading congregations confronting the generational divide.

Still other congregations may find change foisted upon them in the persons of Younger clergy. The arrival of new, young clergy almost always attracts the young families who seek religious education for their children, and may be threatening to Olders who discover that they are expected to be Church School teachers and put up with noisy children in the worship service. Huge conflicts can break out because the older congregation and a younger minister do not share the same worldview, even though each thought they were speaking the same language. These may be hidden in technological communication or interaction patterns that have little to do with age—they have everything to do with worldview differences.

Congregations that are growing or declining are also experiencing generational stresses. If certain generational cohorts are growing in new members, the balance may shift quite suddenly as demographics change. If, for example, a retirement community or senior housing option opens nearby, enough new Silents or Builders may arrive to destabilize the very congregation they are joining in order to find renewed stability in their own lives. If new housing developments, or a rash of foreclosures happen in the neighborhood, other cohorts may quickly increase or decrease in numbers.

In the face of such huge social change and demographic challenge, congregational leaders must begin the process of educating their congregations about the six-cohort reality. This will not be easy. Most people's experience will be within their own household or neighborhood, and the common 20-30 year gap between generations in families (depending on socio-economic and cultural circumstances) will deeply influence their own and their congregations' views of reality. Their work-world experience will also affect their perceptions. Neighborhood growth or contraction may make other perceptions more vivid.

Whether or not congregations begin to acknowledge and grapple with six generation reality, it has already begun to affect their lives. Because our congregations are uniquely gifted in multi-generational ministry (think of baptisms, weddings, funerals and holy day celebrations), it will be easy for them to be blind-sided. The gathering of an extended family and friends for a wedding will not apparently look very different than it did thirty or forty years ago (except for fashion changes). But to the discerning eye, it will become clear which cohorts are represented, and which are not. The youngest will probably still be a baby, but the oldest may be 90, with the other four cohorts also present.

Paradoxically—Biblically speaking!—congregations are also blessed places where every member is recognized as a valuable member of the body of Christ, whether an infant or a fragile very-elder. Congregational leaders have an opportunity to re-Vision the church as the authentic place where hard conversations about how we live with multiple generations of adults not only can happen, but must happen! Even the most cynical GenXer may find something other than marketing in a church's plea for tolerance, understanding, and an earnest desire to find "another way" of living together in love, dignity and respect.

How shall we get started in building our own and our congregation's awareness of these issues?

The single most valuable tool for leaders who wish to begin an extended conversation with their congregation to understand these generational dynamics, may be conversation itself. Beginning to have such conversations might be as much as a congregation is able to bear for the first few months, for it will confront the myth that we are "all one family." As differences emerge, and a congregation develops the skills to discuss itself in demographic cohort terms, a sense of grief and loss may develop. There may also be anger at those who are focusing on differences. At some stage, after the realization of difference occurs, a new way to see the congregation as an organic whole with different parts may be necessary.

We need to repeat a warning—there is a great deal of emotion stored in the old three-generational model. Participants in an age-graded, top-down authority system often have to swallow their anger and internalize their frustrations until they finally age/credential into powerful positions: *"I had to wait, so you do, too!"* Some of the resentment of doing this over several decades can produce residual anger that will color relationships and begin interactions in a highly charged emotional context. Other Olders may feel strongly that they had to do all the work in the congregation and it is time for others to pick up the burden: *"I had to do it; now it is your turn!"*

It may be necessary to work through this anger before the generational cohorts can meet together for substantive conversation. Congregational leaders may need to talk these issues over themselves, often with a trained facilitator, until they can understand and accept others' anger—and their own!

After leaders are sure that beginning the conversation will be possible without conflict or accusations, an exercise like the Congregational Discovery Exercise in Appendix I may help map each congregation's own unique pattern of generational cohorts. When leaders come to a deep understanding of their own congregations' particular pattern of cohort membership and who holds "old member" status, some of the conflict areas may become less tense. (This is in quotes because a 40-year-old who has been a member all her life is an old member.) Every congregation will have a different pattern, and there is no correct pattern. If leaders think of this as their own generational fingerprint or DNA analysis, they may be able to reduce some of the emotional loading.

Once you know your own congregational pattern and leaders are able to use the generational cohort terminology neutrally, real conversations can begin. Three areas may be most fruitful for prayerful, slow examination and discernment: worship, Christian formation and programs. In the next two chapters we will explore how worship and Christian formation patterns are being affected by the generational and worldview crises, and what some of the areas for both disagreement and healthy new beginnings may be. Chapter Seven will deal with programs that affect use of resources and the buildings that serve the congregation.

Questions:

1) Did any of the congregational Moments you have read so far seem familiar in any way? If so, was there any one person you sympathized with? Anyone who seemed very unrealistic in his/her expectations?

2) Did you ever notice that only Olders or only Youngers were present at some congregational event? How did you feel about it then? Now?

3) Think about last Christmas or Easter in your congregation: how many cohorts were present? How did it feel to have them together?

4) Are there any generational issues involving preferred communication style among your congregational members? Within the Church Board? With your clergy?

5) How is your congregation handling the question of texting Teens and Tweens?

6) Is your congregation actively involved in social networking? Do the clergy or congregational leaders participate?

Chapter Five

Worship

A Congregational Moment

The clergy of Trinity Church, Father Dave and Assistant Rector Mary, had spent the previous year inviting their congregation to participate in Listening Groups, informal discussions about parish life and the way members felt about many issues. About a third of the congregation had participated, including the Confirmation class youth. Among other topics, they talked about worship and Christian formation/education at Trinity. The quiet traditional service at 8 am, the service at 10 am with music and hymns, and the 5 pm, "come as you are" with contemporary music all appealed to different segments of the congregation, and people said they loved the balance. And yet, Dave and Mary were aware that the youngest members and their families were less and less comfortable with staying in pews during formal worship. There was a growing tension between worship and community, as young parents would take their toddlers out to the sunny large vestibule during the sermon and the quieter parts of the liturgy.

Trinity has always valued community. It is the first core value mentioned in its Mission Statement: *We are a community of Christian people seeking to love God with all of our hearts, minds and strength and to love our neighbors as ourselves."* The strength of their sense of community has allowed this congregation to feel free to explore many forms of prayer, music and fellowship. The Listening Group reports seemed to suggest that Trinity was ready to experiment with different liturgical forms in order to provide appropriate worship for all its members. So—during Lent the following year, Trinity's Liturgy Committee created a different, but simultaneous service in the attached Parish Hall. It was introduced as a community exploration, a Koinonia (from the Greek, meaning fellowship, sharing and community) Liturgy. (Say: coy-nuh-nia)

The announcement said "For five Sundays in Lent, a Koinonia worship service will take place . . . **simultaneous** to 10:00 am traditional Lenten worship in church. There will be **no** church school during these five weeks. The new service has been designed to be interactive, with dramatization of the gospel. It calls for active participation of the people gathered in all aspects of the service. This service is appropriate for all ages. Families are encouraged to stay together whether they choose to worship in the church or in the parish hall."

The Parish Hall was arranged with four seating groups—two seating groups on each side of a central table dressed in altar linens with the chalices, patens, bread and wine resting on top. A piano was at one end of the room, and a small prayer table with cups of colored "prayer sand" was at the other. Art depicting parts of the gospel hung on a temporary wall behind the prayer table. The service was designed to be both a simple Episcopalian Eucharist, and an interactive intergenerational worship service that engaged all the participants' senses. Instructions were given briefly before and during the service. The Gospel was presented by different lay teams each Sunday, and music was simple, combining contemporary and traditional hymns. The whole service was printed in a large-type booklet.

Participation and shared experience were key to worship. As persons offered their own prayers they were each invited to pour some colored sand into a large clear glass vase, thus building a community prayer vessel. One child was invited to serve the communion bread and one adult the communion wine at each of the four seating groups, so that eight people were involved in serving each Sunday. The gospel presentation teams included multiple age groups each Sunday. The traditional Lenten service, with organ, choir and sermon was held in the sanctuary at the same time. The clergy alternated officiating at each.

The Koinonia service first attracted about forty people, primarily young families (GenX parents and GenZ children) with a few Boomer grandparents. Over the five weeks of Lent, attendance slowly grew to about 85, which was about as many people as the space could handle. Many parishioners tried the Koinonia service once. The Boomers and Silents usually went back to the traditional Lenten service, unless they had family members participating in Koinonia. The children thoroughly enjoyed this style of worship. The question was: is this child-appropriate worship, or is it something larger?

Dave and Mary were aware that they were raising issues about worship and expectation, so they had a short "debriefing" session immediately after each Koinonia service, to ask people what they thought, what they particularly liked, and what might have been difficult for them. After Lent they had one more Koinonia service, and then asked the whole congregation, several times after Easter: "What if this was a regularly held service?"

To their surprise, while all the younger parents liked it very much, they missed the organ, the processions, the choir-led hymns, and the beautiful, traditional worship in the sanctuary. They were concerned that they were splitting Trinity's strong community, and they wanted their children to experience traditional Episcopalian worship. One of the GenXers explained: "Church is the one thing that is stable in my life. I want it to continue to be, and I want my kids to experience the church that way."

While Dave and Mary have tried to incorporate the "prayer sand" into the traditional service, they note with regret that now children tend to be a bit more reluctant to participate, unless specifically invited; yet all ages have expressed attraction to this concrete action as a form of prayer. And the GenX parents still tend to take their noisy little ones out to the vestibule during the sermon. While they are wrestling with these issues, they are clear that six generational cohorts create a new challenge for their congregation. As they reflected, they said: "Trinity Church is not resting—we continue to explore God's call to share the Good News in Christ."

The key to understanding what happened at Trinity Church is contained in the second word of their Mission statement: *Community*. Congregations that embrace community as their primary core value are the most likely to be able to create authentic multi-generational events and worship, no matter what their liturgical tradition. When this happens, community can even trump worship, as the members find engagement with each other of higher value than almost any other bond.

The children (the youngest Millennials and GenZers) clearly preferred the Koinonia service and their participation was high. The formal architecture of rows of pews facing the altar and pulpit in the church proper was not as conducive to participation in the gospel discussion or the "sand prayers," as it was active in the Koinonia setting. But young parents want to be full-fledged members of the congregational community—in the church—even more than they want to be participants themselves or with their children in another setting.

Such community-focused congregations tend to have other similarities. When the congregation is growing and relatively new (younger than fifty years) and continuing to function in a single multi-purpose worship and fellowship space, the necessity of doing worship, events, and all-congregation meetings within the same space creates its own multi-generational dynamics. If the fellowship space is physically contiguous to the worship space, some of the same dynamics exist.

Because there is "no where else to go" and "we all have to learn to get along with each other," healthy congregations which are growing—even by natural increase as the babies arrive—must find ways to make psychological and physical room for the multiple cohort differences. Ironically, as the community expands, the very thing they did not want inevitably happens—different cohorts find physical spaces and social places for themselves. One of the pressures that will rip these congregations apart is the very natural growth they experience. And if they refuse to provide additional physical space, they will begin to get locked into the old three generation model, which will start to proclaim: there isn't enough space for "them."

When these congregations take a long time (years—even a decade) to discern that they need more space, and move slowly through the process of recognition, design, raising the money and building larger quarters, they emerge with large building facilities and a stronger sense of themselves, without losing their core value of community.

To return briefly to Trinity Church, its clergy's refusal to stay with one experiment or one model will continue to push the congregation to explore how to make the six-cohort society's needs for God and worship in a multi-generational community function. As they do this, maintaining multiple open lines of communication will be essential to maintaining Trinity's strong sense of community.

Not every congregation feels the need or the freedom to experiment with their worship patterns. For many Christian churches that come from strong liturgical traditions, participation in the annual liturgical cycle forms a core value. The Advent-Christmas-Epiphany-Lent-Easter period may be full of family and congregational traditions that unite the participants in decades of shared memories, music and foods. But these observances may also be barriers to those who do not share their language or significance. In fact, newcomers may be baffled by the congregation's apparent dependence upon them. Youngers may not see why attending all four Sundays in Advent and watching one more candle being lit in the Advent wreath makes any difference at all.

It is worth noting again that many people forty and under simply do not know how to "go to church" or have any understanding of the traditional Christian calendar. Their occasional brushes with liturgy may leave them confused and vaguely resentful that *"every else seems to know what is going on—but I don't."* Their parents may not have been observant, or they may have dropped off their children for Sunday School or weeknight Christian education classes. These now adult competent Youngers know how to take a plane flight, make hotel reservations, go to a restaurant and start businesses, but they may deeply fear attending a church service when they do not know what to do. Weddings and funerals may be the extent of their exposure to formal religion.

Youngers will tell you that they are spiritual but not religious. Often what this means is that they have put together bits and pieces of various spiritualities and have formed a private belief system. They may have spent hours or days testing it and refining it, or it may lie dormant until a life-crisis causes them to look more deeply into themselves and their beliefs. Not having a formal religious context for many of their practices, they are as likely to depend on meditation techniques learned in yoga class as they are on occasionally encountered liturgical practices. Others may have been raised in a church-based tradition of faith and want this for their children. For many, megachurches with their active social calendars provide attractive entry points, simply because so much "church time" is filled with social activities and service projects. Other large congregations may also have the resources to have significant numbers of Youngers to form critical mass. When this happens, Youngers will self-organize activities that interest them, and may well fill their "church time" with social events or service activities for themselves and their families. It is not unusual for these folks to attend worship rarely, even though they may be very active in non-worship activities.

Medium size congregations may have the hardest time in balancing Older and Younger issues and attracting Youngers to worship. The most common strategy is to focus on children and have a family-friendly service sometime between Saturday evening and Sunday evening. These usually include shorter, simpler worship forms, participatory music and prayers, and a brief homily rather than a full sermon. Often children read prayers or lead singing. Non-related Olders rarely attend (except those who come for the fun of seeing small children) and they may be quite distressed at the sight of toddlers and pre-schoolers sitting on the altar steps, crawling under the altar or pews, or doing other kid things. The most successful and growing Younger worship services allow parents and children to participate with minimal need for previous knowledge.

The challenge for clergy and congregational leaders in more traditional churches is to carve out a psychological and social niche for Youngers who are not traditionalists, but who yearn for a church community for themselves and Christian training and formation for their children.

A Congregational Moment

Pastor Jim was worried. For years, there had only been two worship services on Sunday: a small, quiet 7:30 service that was liturgically correct, but spare, and a large service at 10:30 with choir and music. Most of the people who attended early worship were in their 50's, 60's and 70's, plus a few younger people who worked on Sunday and could get to church first if the sermon was short. The main service (he always thought of it that way) used to be full of children, parents and grandparents, but several years ago he and the Parish Governing Council gave in to the pleas of younger families for an earlier, child-friendly service that would allow them to participate in sports on Sunday too.

Pastor Jim could scarcely refuse—he'd baptized some of these young parents. So the Assistant Pastor and he decided that they could do a simple worship service at 9 am. The Assistant would lead the Family Service while he taught the Adult Formation class. It had proved to be a good decision. After the ten young families started going to the 9 am service and the regulars got used to their absence, attendance only slowly slipped at the main service. That had more to do with people getting old, dying and moving away, than anything else. And the Family Service grew and grew. Sometimes there were 80 or 90 people attending now.

But the Assistant was leaving to take a new call, and the budget was down for the coming year by 18%. New families were not giving very much, and several major donors—the most faithful tithers—had died. Pastor Jim knew that the congregation could not afford to replace the Assistant Pastor's position, and he did not have the physical energy to do both a third service and the Adult Formation class, even if he could be in two places at once.

After Alyssa, the Parish Governing Council president, announced that there would have to be serious cuts in their congregation's programs, several congregants came to see Pastor Jim about what that would mean.

Bill, a young man in his thirties with two little girls, was adamant that the 9 am service must not be changed in any way. "I struggle to get my wife to come to church," he said. "It's only because our girls love coming that she began attending regularly."

On the other hand, Carolyn, a grandmother, suggested that "This is the time to get that 9 o'clock service back under control. I did not want to say too much while our nice Assistant was here, but really! Those children are allowed to run wild. They have no manners and no one makes them be quiet or stay in the pews. Do you know that they make a big circle around the altar during Holy Communion, and the children are permitted to crawl on the floor?

"Pastor," she said: "Many of us think it is time to combine the 9 o'clock service with the 10:30 service before an entire generation grows up in total disrespect."

Pastor Jim could understand both sides of the issue. He secretly agreed with Carolyn, whose opinion he respected. But Bill clearly spoke for the younger families. Luckily, his Council President was a woman in her mid-forties who seemed to be able to get along with everyone. Alyssa was in charge of marketing for a very successful tech company, and had recently convinced even the oldest member of the Parish Governing Council to move to e-mail communication. (He would always wonder how she did it so easily!) Pastor Jim was deeply impressed by Alyssa's ability to communicate well with the whole congregation. He suspected she even knew the names of all those new people at the 9 am service, for she often attended it.

That evening, as they sat in his office they considered what to do.

Pastor Jim and Alyssa have some very hard decisions to make, and they need to identify their congregation's core values realistically before they make them. They will also need to know their own congregation's pattern of cohorts. How many cohorts do they have in each worship sub-community? How many members overall do they have in each cohort? What representatives from those cohorts sit on the Parish Governing Council?

If they take the time to do this basic homework, some clues about how to find appropriate resolutions may appear. If they do not do this work, conflict is almost guaranteed. The range of options is daunting. Would it be best to move Christian formation for adults to a weeknight or Saturday morning small-group meeting? Would it make more sense to combine two of the services? Which two? Would it be better to find a clergy or lay leader to lead the 9 am service? Or would that only widen the generational split that seems to be growing in the congregation? Yet the 9 am service will soon be the largest service if its growth continues for another year or two. Surely something good is happening to bring all those young people to church with their children!

What Pastor Jim brings to their discussion are the almost intuitive gifts of long ministry in a single congregation. His leadership has been very good, balancing both administrative flexibility and compassionate pastoral care. His decision to hire an Assistant has resulted in excellent growth among younger families, but he is about to have to make some very hard choices in the light of a major budget cutback. Perhaps the answer is for him to retire and let a younger person lead this congregation. If he could just hire another Assistant!

What Alyssa brings to the table are good business skills and leading-edge GenX "translation" abilities. As the oldest child in her family, she knows the Silents and Boomers well, and appreciates their traditional strengths. But she also knows that her younger GenX siblings and her own Millennial children see the world differently. She will be quick to assure Pastor Jim that trying to combine the 9 am and 10:30 services is a recipe for conflict and people leaving. She sees that Pastor Jim is wondering whether he should leave—what a loss that would be. If she could just figure out how to hire another Assistant!

This kind of dilemma is being played out in congregation after congregation across our country. There are no easy answers. During the ten or twenty years that will mark a clear transition from Olders to Youngers and the resolution of the generational divide, dozens of response strategies will be tested. While not simply a matter of financial resources, some of these strategies will be affected by the Great Recession. Its pressures will hasten some congregations' closing or merging, and change the role of clergy in many others.

One response is the sort of congregational conversation that we discussed in Chapter Four. Another might be to actively seek to augment the staff with part-time clergy or lay ministers. Recently retired and bi-vocational clergy may add educational or worship leadership resources until finances improve. Yet another would be to seek a companion congregation or merge with a smaller one. By sharing resources, two full-time clergy may be able to continue to serve the combined congregations.

Many congregations have decided to rent out space to other small congregations—often of dramatically different denomination and worship styles, and of different ethnic makeup. Some see this as a ministry of sharing resources; others just want the rental fees to shore up dwindling budgets.

No matter what the strategic response, it will have large implications for the on-going life of the congregation(s). Careful analysis of generational factors may bring insights that would be otherwise hidden. Would a congregation that is mostly Olders see a small struggling congregation of other Olders as competition? Would they accept a small congregation of young families from another cultural or worship tradition as people to be sheltered and cared for? Would a congregation with a few Olders and several GenX young families accept a medium-size mostly Boomer congregation as a building or worship partner?

Making such decisions must be part of a long-term discerned response, and not the arbitrary decision of the Pastor or top leaders. It is worth finding ways to slow down the action to make such broad, whole-congregation conversations possible. Reading books like John McDonald's *Who Stole My Church* and Carol Howard Merritt's *Tribal Church* together may help congregational leaders discern the correct strategy for their own particular congregation.

In any case, you may be relieved to know that Pastor Jim and Alyssa were able to find a third-year seminary student who wants to obtain experience in children's worship to fill in at the 9 am service while they figure out what to do.

Congregations are natural multi-cohort gathering places—sometimes!

As we noted in Chapter Four, Christian people of all ages gather naturally for certain worship and life-transition services: Christmas, Easter, baptisms, weddings and funerals. Such celebrations may temporarily unite in harmony members of all six cohorts. To the Olders, these are reassuring reunions of families and friends coming together in appropriate and approved ways. To the Youngers, they are un-marketed, un-mediated authentic gatherings that offer real spiritual content.

There are certain notable differences about these services. Because many people who do not know "the rules" are expected, service leaflets are usually extensive and guide participants through the service more completely than they may on an ordinary Sunday. Children and newcomers are usually given wide latitude in expectations about their behavior. The most widely known music is played and sung. There may be a special anthem offered by the choir, and additional instrumental or choral performances may be included. It is rare that any group will be segregated, but formal childcare may be provided. If there is food, it will usually be special and in larger quantities than on ordinary Sundays. Multiple-cohort pre-events or post-events are also likely to happen around such occasions, and even those that may be cohort-specific, such as a Christmas pageant or Easter egg hunt, are meant to be enjoyed by all ages.

There are differing styles about communication and planning that also need to be negotiated. When gatherings are arranged electronically, they are more fluid, spontaneous and shared then when they are scheduled into a physical space weeks or months ahead. GenXers and Millennials are very comfortable with this electronic planning. Olders tend to prefer scheduled planning unless they know all the players very well already.

Many weddings today are a hybrid form of event, as they make it necessary for long-term scheduling to happen. This makes Olders quite comfortable, but they cannot understand why engagements and weddings are sometimes years apart. GenXers and older Millennials make sure that the date is so far ahead that there can be no question about their Tribe's ability to attend—and participants take vacation time to do it. They also try to make it a Tribal experience, with multiple days of parties in an attractive location, as their tribe assembles from many directions. Choosing the church and clergy is often secondary to nabbing the perfect wedding setting, reception location, and appropriate housing and weekend entertainment for guests. At the same time, the gatherings are very likely to include family members of all ages, which build on-the-ground community.

To a minor degree, baptisms and funerals follow a similar pattern. The growing attraction of the Memorial Service certainly reflects the need for family and friends, if not tribe, to assemble with sufficient notice from places far away. Clergy and congregational leaders, once again, have to negotiate the physical realities of distance and their desire for Christian community. Dr. Thomas Long's book, *Accompany Them with Singing*, reflects the tension inherent in the modern Christian funeral. When people of all ages are gathered with a shared purpose in the name of God, the church is offered an opportunity to be at its best.

These elements of shared Christian purpose combine to make such multi-cohort gatherings enjoyable. By and large, congregations understand how to make them so. The question is: why don't they do this all the time? Some of the generational divide issues we discussed in Chapter Three may need to be reviewed in the light of your own congregational worship experiences.

Questions:

1) Once again, did you find yourself resonating with a particular person in any of the Congregational Moments in this chapter? If so, why?

2) In the first Congregational Moment of Chapter Five, does Trinity Church's failure to establish a permanent Koinonia service bode well or ill for its future? How does your own congregation balance community coherence and age-appropriate worship formats? Do Millennials regularly participate in the conduct of worship in your congregation?

3) What would you advise Pastor Jim and Alyssa to do in the second Congregational Moment? Do you think that using a seminary student will work? What do you think about Pastor Jim's not knowing many of the new young families at the 9 am service? Has this congregation actually become two churches housed under a single roof?

4) Do you know of other congregations which have tried varying worship formats to meet generational cohorts' desires? Are they large, medium or small congregations?

5) What worship style do you prefer? What do your parents prefer? Your children? What draws multiple cohorts?

6) Do you have one or more all-cohort worship events during the year? What is distinctive about them? What stands in the way of your incorporating some or all of their characteristics into your ordinary worship practices?

Chapter Six

Christian Formation

The Christian tradition of faith formation is a very ancient one, with roots in the Hebrew Scriptures. We received faith and religious instruction from our ancestors and pass it along to our descendants. In the Catholic and Protestant traditional understanding of faith, there is an expectation that one's family of origin is the first source of religious training, with formal teaching about more complex issues coming through formal education, the congregation and clergy as one grows up.

Give ear, O my people, to my teaching;
incline your ears to the words of my mouth.
I will open my mouth in a parable;
I will utter dark sayings from of old,
things that we have heard and known,
that our ancestors have told us.
We will not hide them from their children;
we will tell to the coming generation
the glorious deeds of the Lord, and his might,
and the wonders that he has done. (Psalm 74:1-4)

For I received from the Lord what I also handed on to you, that the
Lord Jesus on the night when he was betrayed took a loaf of bread, and
when he had given thanks, he broke it and said, 'This is my body that is
for you. Do this in remembrance of me.' (1Corinthians 11:23-24)

Part of the Law given to the people of God contained instructions about their responsibility to teach future generations about God and the life of the community. Likewise, since the time of Paul, one of the chief responsibilities of the Christian Church has been to pass on the faith to our children. The Episcopalian rite of ordination (*Book of Common Prayer,* p.531) for example, calls for leaders of the church to be pastors, priests and *teachers.* Yet increasingly, churches are finding that the programs of Christian Education/Spiritual Formation that served them well as recently as 10 or 15 years ago are no longer working.

Part of the explanation about why so many churches are struggling to find ways to provide education/formation may be generational. From the nineteenth century onward, in the tried and true three-generation model, Olders understood it to be their responsibility to teach Youngers, and expected (as did the Youngers) that when the Youngers became parents themselves, they would then become teachers for their own children, while the Olders would move on to classes taught by the pastor, or perhaps become teachers of Adult Sunday School classes. The typical "Sunday School Hour" of the last century consisted of classes for adults and a graded Sunday School in which parents (usually, but not always women) taught the children.

Sometimes children's classes were held during worship, with children leaving to go to Sunday School class while adults stayed for Communion. More recently the liturgical model has shifted so that children join the worship service at Communion having had their class time during the earlier part of the service. In non-liturgical congregations, other patterns occurred, but nearly always involved parents teaching age-graded classes of children. There was an understanding that just as their parents' generation had served as Sunday School teachers for them, now they were to be the teachers of their children's generation.

Several generational issues have made this parents-as-teachers-of-faith model less and less successful—shifts that leave both Olders and Youngers frustrated with one another, and troubled by the expectations each have of the others. One, and often more, of these factors may be at play in churches which are finding it ever more difficult to sustain Sunday School programs.

First, as we have noted elsewhere, church demographics have changed. Many of the parents of young children who make up our congregations did not grow up with the model assumed by the Olders—that is, they did not themselves attend a Sunday School that was taught by their parents and parents' friends. Many were dropped off for Sunday School or weekday Christian Formation classes by non-attending parents. Others now live far away from the generation that taught them. They come as young families to church with no direct ties to the teaching traditions of the Olders. For many Youngers, there is no "tradition" of passing on the faith to the coming generation. Our Olders, by contrast, can't figure out why the Youngers are failing to honor the tradition that for them is still quite real and apparent.

For many Youngers, the tradition and expectation of passing on the faith to one's own children is NOT apparent. In many cases, parents of young children may not have attended worship or Sunday School *at all* as children. Many Youngers are coming to our churches for the first time as adults, often attracted by worship, music, outreach programs, or a desire to provide "something more" for their children—something they did not have growing up.

As a result, the parents of our Sunday School aged children do not feel that they themselves have the necessary educational or spiritual background to be teachers. Without having had their own Sunday School education, without having read the Bible, without the formational experience of worship and community (or worship and religious education in *this particular community*), many parents simply feel inadequate to the task of teaching the faith to their children. That's why they are coming and bringing their children, after all! If they were able to provide faith formation for their own children, they wouldn't be here!

A second generational element is closely connected to the first. There is a growing generational divide in the understanding of what it means for parents to raise their children. Olders grew up in a world where they were taught by their own parents, and learned their parents' expertise, with perhaps the aid of a small set of other adults, say the neighborhood piano teacher, the Boy Scout master (who was himself probably the parent of one of the boys in the troop). Today, parents of young children inhabit a world where knowledge and skill are increasingly specialized, and are the domain of highly trained or particularly talented "experts." They themselves were raised by a series of experts, from daycare professionals to teachers and guidance counselors, sport coaches and psychologists. Many would not consider themselves qualified to teach religious knowledge, and they may actually know very little of it. This is part of a larger pattern of responsibility shift for children's education.

Many Younger parents did not learn to cook and sew from their mothers. They did not learn to fix the kitchen sink or change the oil in the car from their fathers. Olders would expect this to have occurred—including the gender-role assumptions that are part of such a pattern. The loss of that rigidity is perhaps a good thing, but it does contribute to the breakdown of parent-as-teacher competencies by which general and specific knowledge was transmitted from one generation to another.

This difference in understanding among generations of how we raise our children to become adequately skilled and knowledgeable adults is another generational divide. The model from Psalms and Deuteronomy no longer pertains. It has been replaced by a model in which the teaching and formation of the coming generation is put in the hands of (or purchased from) an array of non-related professional adults who are at the top of their particular field, or at least deemed to be competent by parents. Instead of being their children's teachers, today's parents fulfill their obligation to provide their children knowledge and skill by providing them with a series of tutors, each of whom trains the child in the field in which he or she has gained a particular competency.

From the point of view of Youngers, there is no reason that the institutional church should not be part of the array of people and institutions with whom they contract to form and educate their children. They expect, therefore, that clergy will be religious professionals, trained with at least some graduate level training. Even in those denominations which raise up preachers and clergy from within the congregation, there is usually an expectation that ordination will be followed by advanced education. Lay members also are expected to have advanced training that will qualify them as faith and Bible-teaching professionals. If Olders operate under a paradigm of Christian Formation that says:" *If we don't teach our children the faith, who will?*" Youngers operate under a paradigm that automatically assigns responsibility for faith formation to a set of experts who are not themselves.

A third generational issue concerns the content of teaching. Olders experienced and now expect that children will memorize at least the Lord's Prayer, the commandments and some Bible passages. A Catechism of questions and answers to be memorized was part of many Olders' Sunday School or weeknight religious training. If they attended a denominational school, memorization was part of the curriculum. The role of the teacher was to introduce, explicate the text, and enforce memorization. Reading or telling stories from the Bible was used almost as a reward after formal recitation was over.

Youngers, now accustomed to being able to look up whatever is in question electronically, see less and less need to memorize anything. Stories of kids unable to call their parents because they have lost their cellphone with its preprogrammed autodial—and have no idea what the phone number actually is—are funny but instructive. Youngers also have never experienced the need to memorize large blocks of text or poetry in school, and don't see much point in their children's being forced to do so.

Yet another generational difference revolves around educational style. Instead of the Olders' experience of age-graded, top-down authority in silent classrooms, Youngers have experienced team-based, table or educational center experiential learning. Nearly all classrooms now have teacher's aides and learning specialists of some sort. A single teacher standing in front of students lined up in rows is rapidly disappearing from our society, and strikes many Youngers as contrary to their preferred learning style. When Olders try to enforce this model, both young parents and their children quickly react negatively, either by behavior or absence. When Olders object to cellphones and texting devices being used in classrooms, Youngers may be nonplussed: *How else can they stay connected to their kids?*

An interim strategy has been tried by many denominations, which have developed team-based experiential-learning religious education programs. And they are somewhat successful. But Youngers have to attend training classes in order to be part of the teaching team, and they have to be willing to show up with their children every week, in order to complete the year-long program. GenXers and leading edge Millennials are just not prepared to do that. For many, once-a-month attendance at church seems quite adequate, given all the other demands on family time.

Thus a fifth generational issue has to do with what constitutes committed membership. Recently a Lutheran Pastor had to be in contact with the families of those youth who were preparing for Confirmation, because the parents simply could not manage to have their children present every week for training. He pointed out that they were allowing their children to play many more hours of computer games each week than they were assuring them of religious education before their "adult" commitment to Christianity. He was criticized by Youngers for being harsh, while being praised by Olders in the congregation for reinforcing standards.

Olders, as we have said, come from a world where regular, scheduled face-to-face interaction shows commitment and respect. Youngers experience continuous communication, have little tolerance for repetitious scheduling and live in a world overloaded with sensory input and little time for whole-family interaction.

A Congregational Moment

Assistant Pastor Jerroll would have laughed out loud (or maybe started to cry) if he dared. Cynthia, the Head of Sunday School, was having a meeting for prospective Sunday School parents in the congregation. She told him that she hoped she would be able to recruit several of them to teach, as there were several open classrooms, and asked him to attend in case a few showed interest in teaching and wanted to talk at the same time.

Cynthia was trying to explain Sunday School's importance in forming character to a group of young parents in their late twenties and early thirties, and was having a rough time of it. Unfortunately, she had begun by describing what her own Sunday School training had been like, and how she had learned about respect by sitting in classes where the teachers had impressed her with their unwavering commitment to Biblical knowledge and faith. Year after year she had advanced through the classes, earning attendance medals and good conduct certificates. These were proudly framed by her mother and hung in her bedroom. Cynthia did not seem to notice that the more she described, the less attentive her listeners became.

She looked distinctly unhappy when two mothers picked up their phones and checked the readout. One walked out of the room. A young father left with his baby when it became obvious the child needed changing. Finally she finished her presentation, and asked whether there were any questions. Brooke raised her hand and asked: *"What sort of educational credentials do your teachers have?"*

Pastor Jerroll is going to have a tough meeting with Cynthia sometime soon. She would probably have felt disrespected to the point of rudeness by the Youngers at the meeting, and be hurt that she was treated as she was. After having spent a lifetime earning her position as Head of Sunday School, she will be bewildered about several things:

Why did people simply walk out without even saying "excuse me"? Why would a man bring a tiny baby into a meeting like that? How could that young woman, Brooke, ask such a question? Was she questioning the teachers' faith? Was she trying to be insulting? Who did she think the teachers were? Was she questioning Cynthia's own right to hold her position in the congregation?

By now, you can guess what some of the underlying issues are, and how difficult it will be to explain to Cynthia not only what happened, but why. It may in fact, never be fully possible. It may be equally difficult to explain to Brooke why she should not have asked her question, or at least not in the way she did.

The challenge for congregational leaders is not just explanatory, of course—it is how to rebuild the body of Christ within the congregation in a postmodern, post-denominational world where named position is simply a point in an ever-changing landscape. Both Olders and Youngers are trying to find the security of a Christian community for themselves and their families, but they are asking radically different questions about how it will happen. Olders know why they and their ancestors sacrificed to build classroom spaces for their children. Youngers think it is fine that such spaces exist, but are not sure that they or their children really need to spend a lot of time in them. They are far more concerned that their children see Christian values at work in their world in ways that make sense to them and that they can apply. And they want to be part of the experience themselves. They have so little time with their children that the idea of sending them off to separate classes—yet again—is fairly unattractive. Of course, if the parents have their own activity with good coffee and conversation about living their own lives as Christians, they'll consider letting the teachers have them for another hour!

Congregations are finding many different ways to deal with this vexing problem. Denominational traditions that emphasize everyone's attendance at Christian Formation classes on Sunday morning in ways that nurture supportive small group identities may be having fewer problems than some others. The key concept seems to be community. Congregations that learn how to create and sustain holistic small groups for multiple cohorts—even when the cohorts are separated by age—are finding that Christian Formation forms a natural part of their time together. Where there is a highly mobile, transient population, Youngers may also look to a whole congregation as the source of safe new friends and social relationships, as Olders always have.

Yet Olders and Youngers may define community quite differently. Olders expect their church relationships to carry out and forward into the business, social and even political world. *"I'd like to introduce a friend from church"* means more than an acquaintance in the Older's world. It identifies a certain congregation, with certain socio-economic characteristics and defined beliefs. A *friend* is being vouched for. Such a person comes with implied credentials.

Youngers have tribal friends and social network friends. They introduce people casually, because there are so many, with such differing backgrounds, that who can know who will hit it off? And who can guess who will show up for any given event? And it doesn't really matter, because they're already electronically networked with the people they care about. What congregational life offers them and their kids is authentic community around shared beliefs and the opportunity to gather and talk about them in a safe environment.

Christian formation for Youngers must take into account a common level of ignorance about traditional Christian and Bible literacy, but must never doubt that Youngers are also struggling with life's biggest questions. A congregation's willingness to teach the basics to adults in a non-condescending, non-marketing manner will mark it as respectful. At the same time, congregational leaders must acknowledge that our Youngers will be making ethical decisions about medical service delivery, genetic research, gene modification and cloning, sharing the planet's limited resources, environmental degradation and other critical issues that will affect all of Creation for the rest of history. Clergy and lay leaders' ability to create a sense of welcoming hospitality to newcomers and engage whole-family/ shared households in faith experiences will mark the congregations that thrive in the coming years. Many Youngers are eager for Christian insights about the redemption and salvation of God's Creation through love—called The Good News.

Questions:

1) Which of the five generational issues seems most important to you in fostering a children's Christian formation program in your congregation: parents-as-teachers-of-faith, child-rearing styles, educational content, educational style or committed membership?

2) If you were designing a Christian Formation program for your own cohort, what would it look like? What did your parents' look like? What is your congregation now using?

3) What role does the creation of an all-cohort Christian community have in your congregation's educational programs? What would attract members of your "missing" cohorts?

4) What advice would you give Assistant Pastor Jerroll in the "Congregational Moment"?

Chapter Seven

Programs and Space

A Congregational Moment

Pastor GenX suspected that he was facing a major crisis in his "old suburbs" congregation. This past week Edna had come to tell him that after 30 years, she absolutely had to hand over leadership of *The Lord's Abundance* but no one was qualified to manage it, or willing to learn how to run it. "After all," said Edna, "We designed our food program to integrate with state and federal food programs. We do not allow just any one to get food. They must prove that they are qualified to receive it. We follow the Department of Agriculture food group guidelines in what we distribute to each household. We pack our bags very carefully, and keep thorough records."

Pastor GenX groaned inwardly, but kept a look of sympathy on his face. The town had changed so much since Edna and her friends began the program! While they had done years of wonderful service, there had been complaints from younger members who had tried to volunteer, only to be rebuffed. They saw no reason for the extensive recordkeeping, for income-qualifying the recipients or for prepacking the food bags—especially with items that the recipients might not want or use. And why no fresh vegetables, they asked? Why was the program limited to a few dozen people once a month? Who was being excluded? And why did it only have to happen in the congregation's All-Purpose Room? Surely if more people needed food, the program could use other space?

Rather than raise any of those issues, Pastor GenX had asked Edna about potential successors, and why she felt that no one was qualified to lead it. He had sent Lara—who was interested in feeding the hungry. Edna told Pastor GenX that Lara simply was after an emotional relationship with the recipients and did not want to do the background work. "These young women do not understand how to run a well-managed program," she added. "My generation struggled to prove we could do it, and they take it for granted. We use the All-Purpose Room and it is spotless when we leave. We do not allow our clients to leave the prepared area. I do not think they understand that this takes management and organization. Lara seems to think that she can move the program to the church and expand it. Can you imagine the mess to clean up before the Sunday service the next day?"

Another thing was bothering Edna. She felt that the congregation itself was taking *The Lord's Abundance* for granted, as was the Congregational Board. After Pastor GenX made clear that he supported everyone, and repeated that the Congregational Board had endorsed the food program, Edna relaxed a little. "That's good, Pastor, because many women my age feel just the way I do. We have worked very hard to earn the men's respect. It hurts to have the men and younger women unwilling to support us."

How should Pastor GenX respond? Before we return to this story, let's unpack the issues. Edna is in her early eighties: a member of the Silent cohort. Sandwiched between the Builders and the Boomers, she was raised to "put up and shut up." She vividly remembers her teen-age years during the Great Depression and Pearl Harbor followed by World War II in her early twenties. Her mother celebrated Edna's birthday every year with the words: "You were born on the day women got the vote." For Edna, proving that she could manage money, manage an organization, work hard, keep accurate records, lead a major church program and have "something set aside for a rainy day" is part of her identity as a "modern woman." Where others of her generation had shown their abilities in women's organizations, Edna had blazed a new trail for her congregation, founding and successfully running a volunteer food program for 30 years.

When Lara, a relatively new member of the congregation, phoned to say she was interested in volunteering, Edna had been hopeful that she might well be a good successor. It took only a few minutes before problems began to emerge. Lara said she wanted to feed the hungry, not the "qualified." It did not matter, she said, whether people were worthy, it had to do with whether they were hungry. And why limit the program to the number who could fit into the All-Purpose Room all at once? Why not set up stations in church, including fresh produce, and let people fill their bag with whatever they wanted? So what if they did not want all the food groups? Maybe they had diabetes or a food allergy or intolerance. If they needed more space, why not use the church?

The more Lara talked about expanding *The Lord's Abundance*, the more distressed Edna became. As Lara grew more emotional in her description of possibility, the more rational Edna felt she had to become. She attempted to explain the importance of order, organization and compliance with government standards. Finally, she accused Lara of simply wanting to be "Lady Bountiful"—handing out food for her own emotional preening. Their meeting was not a success. Lara left frustrated and resentful. Edna left affronted and feeling very uneasy about younger people's willingness to carry on important ministries.

Pastor GenX now had a tense situation on his hands. Edna was truly looking tired and did need to hand over this responsibility. But she was determined to wait until she could train someone properly, and felt that would take two years. Lara was making noises about either starting a new food program or finding another church where: *"following what Jesus says is more important than asking someone whether they are looking for a job. If they are hungry enough to come ask for food, we should be feeding them."* Use of the parish's buildings had also begun to snowball into an issue as the two women talked with friends—of their own ages. Edna's volunteers were extremely careful to leave the All-Purpose Room ready for its Sunday fellowship programs when the food program finished by exactly 1 pm on the first Saturday of each month. Lara's younger GenX and older Millennial friends had read Sara Miles *Take This Bread*, and saw the church building as an ideal place to run a food ministry.

Luckily Pastor GenX had done some generational theory work with a clergy study group, and was able to apply this knowledge to the growing conflict. He understood that Edna and Lara were not having a personal disagreement so much as a generational one. As he thought about it, he was struck how much each was acting like a stereotype of her cohort, and how little either's perspective made sense to the other. Using the church building was going to be a hard issue for the congregation he suspected. Yet he too had read *Take This Bread*, and wondered whether fresh produce could be added through a local food bank program. He wondered: why couldn't the church itself be used?

Pastor GenX could see that his role must be both to translate and to begin a decisive process for peace. Let's take up the story again, and see how he solved this challenging set of concerns.

A Congregational Moment—continued

Pastor GenX now was sure he was facing a major crisis in the congregation. If left untended, it had the power to force everyone to take sides. The administration of the food program was one thing, but use of the buildings and access by non-members would galvanize nearly all members if a conflict arose. He concluded that he must have a definite date for Edna's retirement, and schedule a celebration of her service to the church. Then he would call Edna's volunteers to be sure they could be there (so they could be honored, too). But first he would ask if Lara was indeed prepared to take over the food program, beginning the first Saturday that Edna was no longer there.

Both those things fell into place. Edna wanted to retire in three weeks, because she had been invited to spend a month with her son and his family at their farm in Kentucky. Lara had just been to a conference with three church friends that featured Sara Miles, and they were bursting with enthusiasm.

Then something happened that made him wonder whether God was taking a hand in this. His phone rang. The new Community Garden in Town Center was successful beyond everyone's wildest imagination, and they were asking all the food distribution programs they knew if each could start taking fresh vegetables—next week. Pastor GenX gulped, and said: "No, but we can in three weeks." After catching his breath, he began to pray for insight. What did he need to do? As the doubts cleared, he saw that two moves were necessary:

1) He looked over the list of potential volunteers Lara had e-mailed. With the addition of fresh food, 10 volunteers now would be needed each week, rather than the previous need for five once a month. So he encouraged the new committee to seek newer members in their thirties and twenties. This would be an ideal ministry for the newcomers to the congregation.

2) He asked the Congregational Board officers who were scheduled to meet with him next week to take time to discuss and understand why the food program was going to change so fast. He also asked the two youngest Board Members to attend. The topic for the meeting would be: *Why are we feeding the hungry?"*

In advance of the meeting, he told them that the local Community Garden program had requested the church to distribute fresh food every week during the summer months. This would mean that there would be some disruption and different use of space. He had talked with the cleaning service, and they were willing to begin their work at 2pm rather than at 11 am. In fact they were pleased, as the changed time would allow them to take on another church in the morning. Finally, he asked all Board members to put the date of Edna's retirement celebration on their calendars.

Pastor GenX understood that Edna and Lara were unlikely ever to understand each other's worldview, and that trying to get them to work at it was probably wasted energy. It might even sharpen the conflict and make the division between the cohorts clearer. Edna might be hurt at not being part of the food program any longer, but she would have accomplished the retirement she really wanted, and would not have to suffer through the partial dismantling and then large expansion of the program. It would simply change into something she did not recognize.

Pastor GenX also intuited that the younger Boomers and older GenXers, with their better understanding of Edna's worldview, might try to find a compromise that would satisfy no one. Edna would feel that any compromise was a criticism of her management, and the GenXers would feel that someone was trying to preach at them, instead of "walking the walk."

Finally, Pastor GenX recognized that the Congregational Board needed reassurance that the Food program was not out of control. Fresh food and new leadership would certainly change it, but good things were happening and Pastor GenX was shepherding them. Volunteers were in place, Edna was retiring and would be respectfully honored when she returned from vacation, fresh food from the Community Garden (a Board member was also on the Board of that project) would be distributed to those who needed it, and the church buildings would be cleaned at a slightly different time but to the same standard by the same company. The two Silents, five Boomers and five GenXers on the Board probably all heard something different in his report—but then they would, anyway.

Is "Program" dead?

Programs are getting harder and harder to run in our congregations—if they are repetitive and regularly scheduled. And at the same time, those that happen annually seem even deader. *Grandma Sue's Cake and Goodie Sale* which has been going on for 39 years is probably no longer well supported, and may even now be a cause of conflict when formerly it drew all the women members together. Nothing seems to be taking its place, because clergy and congregational leaders may not recognize the one-time, nearly spontaneous gatherings that GenXers seem to prefer as "programs."

Clergy and congregational leaders may be deeply frustrated as they try to create youth programs only to have no reservations, no responses, and then among the few who do sign up, no-shows. The number of programs that have been cancelled through lack of apparent interest is legion. Olders are offended. Youngers are sorry they missed it—but . . . . things happens.

A Congregational Moment

Pastor Sue and Madeleine, the Secretary of the Board who did space-scheduling on a voluntary basis, were a bit taken aback when John GenXer announced without warning one Sunday during Sharing Time, that he had a Mission Event in mind for the first Sunday in May—only two weeks away. John said that a mission school in the Southwest needed supplies for their Vacation Bible School in late June, and he had told the mission school that their church could make 50 school bags—one for each student. John had been to the local office supplies store and discovered that crayons, scissors, paper and paste would all be on sale this coming week. He invited everyone to go buy them, bring them to church next Sunday, and then for all the young families to assemble to make the school bags the following Saturday. He would take care of shipping them.

Later, with relief, Madeleine told Pastor Sue: "The Church Hall is open that day! But don't you think he could have checked with me first?" Pastor Sue had some forebodings about this event, but kept them to herself.

The following Sunday John GenX stood up again during Sharing Time and told the congregation that "Mission School Saturday" would be held from 9:30 to noon, and would include a pizza lunch for everyone who attended. Pastor Sue and Madeleine looked at each other again. They did not have to verbalize their thoughts: "Who is supposed to organize this?" (Pastor Sue had a wedding scheduled at 2 pm in the Church and Madeleine was going to be out of town.) But they were more stunned when John said that he had decided not to use plastic bags. Instead, he was hoping that people would buy or bring any fabric they had at home so that bags with Bible themes could be made Saturday morning. Would there be people who could attend and bring their sewing machines? Several women volunteered to help.

On Saturday, Pastor Sue checked the Church Hall at 11 am before she went to see that everything was ready for the wedding. She found some children running around playing tag, 50 stacks of supplies spread out one-by-one on the stage, several women near tears or barely-contained rage as other children tried to use their sewing machines to make school bags, and the mothers sitting together talking over coffee. John GenXer greeted her with the question: "Did you order pizza?" Pastor Sue said, "No" she had not ordered pizza. Perhaps John would like to?

She turned and looked at the scene. Seeing one of the older members sitting in front of her sewing machine who looked calmer than the rest, she asked if Laura would mind being sure that the lights were turned out and the trash put in bags before the group left, as she, Pastor Sue would be conducting a wedding.

"Quite frankly, Pastor, I am leaving as soon as the pizza arrives and the children are eating. So you'll have to ask one of them. Laura gestured at the group of young mothers. "It's about time they take responsibility for this mess." Pastor Sue found John GenX and made the same request. "Sure!" said John. "Someone will do that."

When Pastor Sue got back to the Church Hall at 4 pm that day, she was relieved to see that the trash was bagged, even if it was not put out. The lights were still on in the kitchen. One quick look showed her that it would have to be cleaned up for "Coffee and Conversation" tomorrow. Pastor Sue sighed and got to work. An hour later she turned out the lights and headed home.

On Monday, two e-mails awaited her. One was full of fury from Laura about "the mess on Saturday" and the other was from a new member, a young mother, who expressed her gratitude and delight at finding such a relaxed and welcoming church for herself and her son.

You can probably now pick out most of the generational issues in this Congregational Moment for yourself. The differences in style, worldview, child-raising practices, responsibility, spontaneity and authority should seem fairly clear. Was this a "program" in Olders' sense of the word? Probably not. Did the Youngers feel that it addressed their needs? At least one did, and she appreciated not having to have her child out of her sight, the inclusiveness of the event, its "outreach/service" intentions, having time to talk with other Moms, and the fact that there was food, so she did not have to worry about lunch. For her, it was a very satisfying morning at church—so satisfying that she felt no need to attend worship the following day.

She is not alone. Increasing numbers of Youngers find that attending a program, volunteering for a congregational service or outreach event, or even attending a concert on Saturday evening or Sunday afternoon fills the "church" slot in their monthly calendar. Program and event volunteers may develop a strong identity and fill holistic small group needs for each other that replace regular worship attendance.

Programs in the end are not a substitute for spirituality (even when some programs directly address spiritual issues). But for many Youngers, they provide a more comfortable way to enter a congregational community than worship. Youngers are clear in their preferences for hands-on, experiential service and social justice related activities. As we have noted in several places in previous chapters, many Youngers will tell you that they are spiritual but not religious. Whenever a congregation strikes them as marketing a product, rather than "walking the walk", they are quick to criticize and quick to leave. Congregations that make authentic claims and deliver services for human need, and that provide access to practices that foster spirituality will be far more attractive to Youngers than those who have programs for the sake of having programs.

But what about the larger issues of buildings, their use, and maintenance of the space so that even the most attractive programs may happen there? One of the challenges congregational leaders will face over the coming two decades will be the negotiation of building issues. The Olders who built or whose predecessors built the churches, classrooms and meeting rooms our congregations use today have a pretty good idea of what it costs and how much maintenance it takes to keep such structures in good repair. They value and financially support these sacred spaces where the congregation—the body of Christ—comes together for worship, education and fellowship.

It is less clear that GenXers and leading-edge Millennials do. At least four factors are involved in their apparent ambivalence toward support and care. They have, in general very high levels of debt: for education, for mortgages and home equity loans, and for the credit they have used to live the life that they believed was appropriate until The Great Recession. They are trying both to meet or to pay down that debt and many are raising children, so there is little discretionary money. Secondly, along with the Boomers, they are extremely anxious about employment benefits and healthcare coverage in a very amorphous economy and political climate. Savings levels are increasing across the country in preparation for these expenses and the presumed tax increases that will be necessary to rid the country of a staggering deficit. A third issue is that most Youngers use church buildings a whole lot less than Olders do, and consequently place them lower on the list of causes they give to. (This may not be as true in small churches with strong ethnic or family connections.) Finally, GenXers have inherited from Boomers the sense that someone older than they will take care of these spaces until they need them. Ironically, GenXers now include Boomers (the source of the rebellion against authority) in the Olders group, and assume that they will take care of the institutions they seem to prize. The Builders and Silents who have been paying for maintenance, working on the structures and the grounds that surround them, and leaving bequests for their long-term support, are going to be disappearing in the coming decades. Boomers may or may not pay for maintenance and repair.

Congregations which have found ways to involve multiple generations in work parties and Church Clean-Up Days as a family activity may be able to create a sense of community ownership among Youngers, but it will take intentional planning and recruitment. In the end, we suspect that Youngers will also come to value and preserve the places where they perceive true corporal and spiritual mercies are performed and their providers are spiritually strengthened and equipped.

Questions:

1) Are you beginning to be more confident that you can identify the generational cohort issues as they occur in the Congregational Moments?

2) Have you noticed any generational issues in your own congregation since you began reading this book?

3) Have you tried to explain any of what you have been reading to an Older? To a Younger? To a member of your own cohort? To other congregational leaders?

4) Have you discovered any more sympathy in yourself for generational issues when you meet them in others at congregational events?

5) Have you helped create a six-cohort event in your own congregation? What worked? What did not work?

6) How does your own congregation care for its buildings? Are you aware of an organization called "Partners for Sacred Spaces" which helps congregations identify parts of their buildings that are worthy for public support? See the Bibliography for more details.

Chapter Eight

Community is Congregation

How do we put our generational understanding into play in congregational leadership?

It will not be enough merely to reorganize what we do, either to separate or to integrate the six cohorts. We must also take into account the changing nature of our congregations. The attention of the past centuries has been on a core of regularly-worshiping members. Indeed, most mainline denominations focus on Average Sunday Attendance to define and describe congregational size and dynamics.

The classic descriptions of church sociology, developed by Arlin J. Rothauge in the 1970's, take as a given weekly attendance by a predictable number of congregational regulars. His "family, pastoral, program and corporate-size" models have been taught in seminaries for several decades. But at least since the beginning of the 21st century, Sunday worship attendance has not been the best descriptor of congregational size, vitality or sustainability. As more and more Boomers and Youngers regard worship attendance once a month as maintaining active membership in a congregation, and many attend less often than that, it becomes clear that the 20th century model no longer works.

If we were to make a map (model) of this old understanding, it might look like a bull's-eye target. The core would be the every-Sunday attenders, Church Council members, clergy and fulltime program staff. The next ring might be part-time staff members, occasionally attending members and the geographically distant children and grandchildren of regularly-attending members. In the next ring outward, we might place judicatory clergy and staff, and pledging Christmas and Easter attenders.

The ring outside that might include those who use/rent the building on an established basis: Twelve Step groups, scouts, other congregations, etc. We could continue making rings outward until we had placed everyone with ties to the congregation—but we would still only really count those in the inner circles when we reported our congregational statistics.

Yet some of those in the farthest out rings might actually attend or visit the church more often than those nearer into the center. What about those who participate regularly in educational, outreach or ministry programs, but rarely attend worship? What about service and delivery people who may interact on a daily basis with clergy and staff? What about neighbors who regularly use the church property and grounds, and may care very deeply about their maintenance? What about those who arrive for a meal or food distribution program on a monthly or weekly basis? What about daycare or preschool children and their parents who may be present more often than any but fulltime clergy and staff?

Perhaps it would be better to map those populations with a classic Venn diagram:

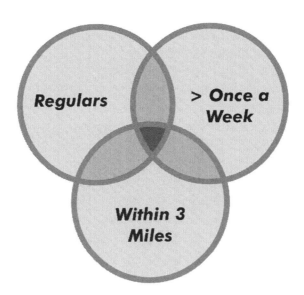

The classic Venn diagram is a simple map of overlapping elements. One example would be: regular worship attenders; people who live within a three-mile radius of our church; and those who use the church buildings more than once a week. Very few people will be in all three circles.

The 20th century insistence that only the Sunday worship regulars should count, is missing the on-the-ground reality of 21st century life. Congregational leaders who allow themselves to be blindsided by history and training will see their church's attendance continuing to shrink, and never pay attention to the perhaps growing numbers of those who interact with the church on a daily or weekly basis.

What right have we to dismiss these children of God as not being "countable?"

The way in which we create a congregational map (model) is the way in which we understand how our congregations actually function in their real world settings. Just as we have mental models for the way in which our families/households function, we all have some sense of the ways in which our congregations function.

It will be worth taking time, after the congregational discussions recommended in earlier chapters, to find out what the mental map of your congregation is. Leaders may discover that there are several maps, not a single shared one. The exercise in Appendix II may help congregational leaders understand how they perceive what is actually present on the ground, and what mental map, or model, other leaders and the congregation as a whole, use to understand their congregation.

A Congregational Moment

Pastor GenX was trying hard to help his Congregational Elders understand what having an increasing number of once-a-month Sunday worship attenders meant for his ability to access Judicatory resources. Faith Church was only half as full on Sundays as it used to be, and the church building needed serious roof repairs. Fifteen years ago, Faith Church had done some other repairs, and was able to get a combination of grant and loan from the Judicatory. But with the economic downturn and Faith Church's dwindling attendance, Pastor GenX could not reassure them that such funding was likely to reoccur.

"Why should attendance matter?" asked the Congregational Treasurer. "Every church in town has lower attendance now. People just don't go to church the way they used to. So we don't get as much in plate offerings and pledges."

"That's right," responded another member. "Our core congregation is actually giving more than they did a few years ago, but the numbers are dropping. We just don't have the number of young families that we used to, and they don't pledge."

"It's because the younger generation is self-indulgent," commented Alice, a woman in her late sixties. "They went out on a limb to borrow more than they could afford, and now they have nothing to contribute to their church."

"Alice," responded David, who just turned 40,"I only finished paying off my education loans last year, and I'm trying to raise two children. My wife and I both work, and we're still paying off her loans, as well as our mortgage. We just don't have much discretionary money to give the church. So we try hard to give back to the church and to the community. We volunteer for the Food Pantry here every other Saturday morning and for Habitat for Humanity once a month—the whole family."

"David" she replied, "I'd much rather see your family in church than working for Habitat for Humanity on Sundays."

"But Alice," David shot back, "Our kids think our community is just as important as our church. We come here several times a month, but we give back to our whole community, too."

Pastor GenX sighed. He did not think he would be able to translate for Alice and David. But he gave it a try.

"Alice and David, both of you are making good points. The problem for our churches is that our world is changing. Alice, you are probably reflecting our Judicatory's view that our Sunday worship attendance should be a deciding factor in whether we receive support. David, I think that most of our under-40 members would agree with you that as people of God, we must regard all God's children as worthy of our assistance.

"If you both will take a look at some passages from the Book of The Acts of the Apostles, you will see that the first believers in Jesus were deeply involved with their community, and that worship occurred both publicly and in peoples' homes."

Pastor GenX had them read Acts 2:42-47, and 4:32-37. Then he asked: "Did you read anything about their only taking care of themselves or only inviting a select group to participate in their ministries? No, they gave to any who had need. The early believers were very much part of their community, and their worship was not organized into specific churches."

"But Pastor" said Alice, "then how did they know who belonged?"

Pastor GenX will struggle hard, and may well not succeed, in trying to help David and Alice understand each other's perspective. He has two separate issues to address: community-as-congregation, and translation between and among generational cohorts.

To help his Congregational Elders begin to grasp the community/congregation challenge of the 21st century, he might invite them to do an exercise like the one in Appendix II. He and they will learn whether the congregation's leaders share the same mental map of the congregation's relationship to its surrounding community.

Congregational leaders can start asking: Who is here on campus regularly? Who gives us support of any kind, and what do we give them? Who are our "stakeholders"—those who have a stake in whether we survive or die? What do they get from our existence, and what do we give them back? If we closed our doors tomorrow, who would notice? Who is our neighbor?

The answers may help leaders see that an exclusive focus on who worships in the building on Sunday morning may also keep them from seeing the many other people who regard this church as an important part of their lives—whether or not they attend worship regularly, or at all. Then the larger issues of community and being God's people may begin to look more like the Book of Acts. Sara Miles' *Jesus Freak* describes St. Gregory of Nyssa Episcopal Church in San Francisco as one where more than 800 people are given free food each week, and people come to faith by participation in the feeding program. It sounds a lot like the chaotic scenes described in *Acts of the Apostles*! No wonder the apostles ordained deacons to take care of the logistics!

Every congregation will have its own style and every community its range of programs, outreach and social justice ministries. What is right for one will probably not be right for another. Yet for each to survive as a vital and growing focus for worship, prayer, service and fellowship, their focus must become larger than Sunday morning attendance.

This leads to the second challenge facing clergy and congregational leaders: translation. Think back to Chapters 2 and 3, where the differences among the worldview of generational cohorts was discussed. While it would be too easy to say that Olders are seeking assurance of grace, and Youngers seeking assurance of love, there is some truth to this. The generational divide makes translation a challenge for the preaching and teaching that form such an important part of Sunday morning church attendance.

Because there is sometimes such incomprehension between Olders and Youngers, the simple message of God's love for the world God created and all that is in it, and Jesus' sacrifice to redeem that world from sin and death, gets lost amid the generation wars. The March 2011 issue of *Philadelphia* magazine pictured a texting device on its cover, with a stark message:

Dear Baby Boomers,
    Just die already. (We'll take Philly from here. Thanks)
    XOXO Generation X

Our GenXers range roughly from 28 to 49 years old in 2011. These are not late adolescents but adults in their first middle-stage, wondering when they get to run the show. Many are already doing it. And many are growing too frustrated to stay in congregations disproportionately populated by and run by second middle-stage adults. And of course, those folks are wondering when they get to be the venerated elders and stop working.

Translation is a harder job than many clergy realize, because we all speak much the same formal language. But the words may mean vastly different things, and new words and text-abbreviations are entering the language all the time. Try using the language of social networks and texting in the pulpit at 8 am on Sunday morning!

Every generation must come to understand the core truths of its religion and to express them in their own words and songs. Certainly every generation in this country has mystified its elders by adopting and adapting new language to describe its understanding of patriotism. If the language of religion has apparently not changed as rapidly, then it may well be catching up and making up for lost time.

What can clergy do to assist in the translation process? Minimally, they must read and listen to all the cohorts as each attempts to express their own understandings of God's love and Jesus' message. Dan Kimball's book, *They Like Jesus But Not the Church: Insights from Emerging Generations*, is so named for a good reason. Every pastor needs to know why he called his book that. Kendra Cressy Dean's *Almost Christian: What the Faith of Our Teenagers is Telling the American Church* is also well named.

Another way is to be sure that clergy and congregational leaders do not isolate themselves by surrounding themselves with people their own age. (If you have not been aware of generational tensions in the last week, you are not where the action is.)

Some of the ways our six generational cohorts are making physical and psychological space for themselves is by broadening the old boundaries. Youngers are less apt to attend regularly. They may regard volunteering for, or participating in, church-related programs as equally filling of their spiritual needs. They want their households and families to be able to do many things together in the limited time available, and if these can also feed them spiritually, even better.

The reality for our Youngers can be deeply frustrating for clergy and denominational leaders who are trained in last century's model. Pastor Boomer wants to see the Youngers and their families at worship, not arriving at 12:30 on Sunday afternoon to eat pizza and participate in a family-friendly outreach event. He may completely miss the fact that for them, they *have* attended church. Congregational leaders may be equally confused by these same Youngers identifying this as their church, and expecting baptisms, marriages and funerals from clergy whom they rarely see.

To the degree that congregational leaders can understand how the generations are living church, tribal and community lives—both face-to-face and electronically—will be the way in which our congregations respond to the actual world in which they live.

What will such congregations look like? They may be as free-wheeling as St. Gregory's or as tight as a family chapel; they may be niche churches for 2 or 3 generational cohorts or intergenerational gathering places deeply integrated with the lives of their communities. What seems clear already is that unless they have substantial endowments, they will only be able to support church buildings to the degree that all their stakeholders (not just the core worshipping members) are willing to support them.

Partners for Sacred Places, a national organization, spent the last two decades showing church and synagogue congregations how to involve their communities in their future *"Partners is the only national, non-sectarian, non-profit organization devoted to helping congregations and their communities sustain and actively use older and historic sacred places"* says their website (*www.sacredplaces.org*). When communities and neighbors become involved in the future of a church or synagogue, and are treated as responsible and important partners in keeping these valuable community resources strong, new resources emerge. Partners for Sacred Places has demonstrated, and taught congregations how to access, community resources that can help congregations maintain and reuse their buildings for community service and outreach.

Yes, authentic welcoming and incorporation of six generational cohorts takes a major change in mindset for all involved. No, it cannot be lip-service that is a poor disguise for merely seeking money to support a core of Sunday worshipers. New members will need to be accepted for a range of attendance and involvement, and only congregational leaders and clergy can decide where the balance should rest for any particular congregation and its relationship to its denominational governance structure.

Congregational leaders who focus on community and the complex relationships among generational cohorts, while teaching, demonstrating and preaching what being a Jesus-follower is really like, will do a better job of keeping churches vital and strong than will number-counting on Sunday morning.

This will require denominational and judicatory shifts of perception that are quite substantial. One clergyperson recently remarked: "If my bishop would agree to let me count the number of people who enter our church buildings and grounds each week, I'd number attendance in the thousands. Instead, because our sanctuary is small, and Sunday worship attendance is slowly shrinking, I look as though I am leading a dying church. But the reality is that we do more real hands-on ministry than the church down the highway that is twice as large."

He is not alone. When asked how many of the people involved in the ministry programs regularly attend worship, he said: "Very few. But many times, they want me to come to their meetings and offer a prayer. They want to be married here and have their funerals here. They call me if someone is in the hospital. They know this is their church and we are ready to care for them if they need help."

Not surprisingly, when a summer storm blew down trees and branches, several neighbors and program-attenders offered to help with the work and expense of the clean-up. They wanted to give back some of the love and support that they had received.

Just as our communities are slowly finding ways to integrate all six generational cohorts into civil society, so must our congregations. The task ahead will be challenging. It will require exciting levels of creativity and thinking outside the box. It will offer those who believe that Jesus has a place in the 21st century fascinating glimpses of him as he walks ahead of us into the future, saying "Fear not!"

Questions:

1) When was the last time you checked to see how many generational cohorts were present at a congregational event? At a neighborhood event (like Halloween, say?) At a community event? Which generational cohorts live in your community? Do they share the space all the time, or do they appear at different times of the day and evening?

2) Have you tried—again—to tell anyone outside your study group about the six-cohort reality?

3) How does your congregation interact with your surrounding neighbors? Are the generational cohorts inside your congregation similar to, or dissimilar to those in nearby houses and apartments?

4) If you walked outside today for a longish walk, which generational cohorts would you see? At the library? In the post office? In the food store? Who walks? Who rides? Which cohorts ride each type of wheeled vehicle?

5) Can you name one thing that each generational cohort in your community particularly wants? Name one thing they especially dislike. Are all cohorts from the same ethnic, cultural or racial groups?

6) Can you name one thing that your congregation could do to make each generational cohort feel welcome and valued in your church buildings and grounds?

7) Have you ever had to "translate" between generational cohorts? Did knowing something about the other cohorts from your generational study in this book help? How?

Chapter Nine

The Way Forward: Love

What is it about these generational differences that should concern us as members of the body of Christ? What has changed? In one sense, nothing at all. We are still linked as Paul understood deeply, as parts of an organic whole. Yet at the same time, the body that is humankind is going through a brain-processing transition as huge as the physiological transformation that is adolescence. If we use biology as a metaphor, we see that all the major brain structures are being rewired, and that our communication and perception processes are undergoing restructuring.

During adolescence, when the hormones begin to fire up in preparation for transforming the child into a sexually mature human and then in the second stage, into a rationally mature human, science tells us that the deep structures of the brain are massively changed. The adolescent experiences shifts in consciousness that transforms her/him from a child to an adult.

If you want another parallel, consider the shift in communication and perception that happened when humans developed writing. Our electronic media now integrate visual, aural and written media in ways that change our brain-wiring. We process integrated electronic information differently than we process printed words on a page.

Today these deep-structure physiological changes are being challenged and augmented by an external technological change. The combination is not linear. It is at least geometric. And beyond that, there is the unpredictable influence of a crisis of human populations and their waste products—by biological standards—that is changing the underlying planetary ecology.

Is it all up for grabs? Is it "the end of the age?"
Where is God in this? Where shall we find Jesus?

The Olders are deeply confused and saddened. All the churchly things that reassured them they were in God's presence have gone away or are being challenged by the Youngers. The music, the liturgies, the sense of proper order and decorum, the reassuring precedence that reasserted social conventions, have gone away or are under attack. Worst of all, the Youngers simply seem uninterested.

The Prophet Elijah discovered that God was listening to him in the sound of sheer silence, after the wind, the earthquake and the fire. He had thought that God would speak to him: instead God was listening to Elijah. God spoke to Elijah in ways that may make us shudder, because they were God's last command to Elijah: "anoint the kings and anoint your successor, Elisha." In other words, Elijah's days were numbered. (1 Kings 19:11-16)

Our role as Olders is to accept that we will be asked to anoint our successors, forgive our failings and leave, like Elijah. Our role as Youngers is to understand that we must take up the mantle of prophecy. We must speak the truth, proclaim the Good News of forgiveness and salvation, and stop being resentful about not receiving rewards from an Older world that is going out of existence.

These two ways of forgiveness must overlap if the Church is to survive and grow into its 21st century promise: a little praise music won't do it for the early service, and a little children's music or sermon won't do it for the later service.

The challenge of worship and formation has to do with an old gospel truth: Jesus came to call everyone to the discipline of love. And that love is different for different people. While God's love may always be unconditional and never-failing, it is not blind. The child may need comfort, the youth challenge. Adults need God's love as guidance and wisdom to make hard choices. At the close of our lives we need the rock that anchors the gateway of death. Elijah needed God's love to leave; Elisha needed a double portion of God's love just to continue in his master's mission. (2 Kings 2:9)

As Elijah's day passed; Elisha's began. As the 20th century becomes memory, the 21st century grows and spreads its new ways of being human. The old values of love do not change. Love will require patience and kindness on all sides. As Paul says in his letter to the Corinthians: those who follow the way of love are not envious, angry or boastful;

they keep no record of wrongs and are not self-seeking. (1 Corinthians 13:4-6)

The way of love will ask Olders to understand that they too must hand over the mantle of prophecy—not knowing what words will be spoken, texted or tweeted, what videos will be made or played. What they can ask is that the Youngers speak truth fearlessly and proclaim Jesus' rule of love to the 21st century.

Love asks the Youngers to deeply respect the sacrifices and struggles of the Olders to preserve the best as their world has fallen apart. Like Elijah, the Olders are stumbling into a desert where all the structures of their faith are being abandoned and disregarded. Wind, earthquake and fire are telling of God's ending one generation and beginning another. What Youngers can do is ask the Olders to speak truth fearlessly and proclaim the core values of Christianity to the 21st century as they hand over the mantle of prophecy.

This will be hard, hard work. Neither will accomplish it well without deep faith that God is working God's purpose out, and we cannot know what that may be. Phyllis Tickle, a church sociologist and writer, says that this transformation is as large a social shift as the Reformation was. It is possibly larger than that, and is as great a shift as the invention of written language. In any case, it will change how, when, and the process by which we worship God.

But it will not change why we worship our Creator. And it will not change the primacy of Love.

God is calling us to live through a time of transition with faith as our guide, and Love as our touchstone. As Olders and Youngers, we must be tender and gentle with each other, for we are Christ's body—together.

A Final Congregational Moment

Pastor GenX's perspective:
   Mark and June's wedding was in many ways very traditional, through some of the Olders didn't see it that way. Both the wedding and the reception were held in the church that they were moving to as a couple, and the fact that the wedding service included five clergy from

different churches and denominations spoke to both the transitory nature of their Leading-edge Millennial lives and their continuing strong connection to each of these faith communities. The praise band, comprised entirely of leading-edge Millennials from yet another church with which they were involved, provided music for the wedding.

At the end of the ceremony, more cell phones than cameras were brought out by the worshipers to capture pictures of the happy couple.

At the reception it became evident how involved all members of the couple's tribe had been in the various details of the day's celebrations: one friend, an avid photographer, gifted them her skills at both the wedding and the reception. Another friend was the videographer. One group of friends decorated the tables and put together an interpersonal scavenger hunt and organized ice-breakers for guests as they waited for the wedding party to arrive. Some of the family offered to do all of the cooking, and another group of friends came together to serve the meal. Even a place to stay for their honeymoon was a gift.

From the outset, this wedding had a communal feel, and this continued in the hours, days, and weeks following the wedding as many of those cell phone pictures popped up on Facebook almost immediately. People around the corner and around the world unable to attend the wedding perused and commented upon the pictures. Some helped by tagging [Facebook term for applying names and links so that those in the pictures can enjoy them and send them to others who might not be able to identify people in them.] Even the newlyweds tagged and commented upon many of the photos while on their honeymoon, thanking everyone and extending the communal excitement while simultaneously perplexing some of the Olders who nevertheless commented with approval how much the whole experience had a good, old-fashioned feeling of community.

Pastor GenX's wife:

"I didn't know Ethan was also at Mark and June's wedding," Pastor Gen Xer's wife said as she was looking through the wedding pictures on Mark's Facebook page. She had been unable to attend the wedding with her husband, but was enjoying 'living' the event through all of the photos that had been posted and tagged on Facebook.

"He wasn't there; at least I don't think he was there. I didn't see him." Pastor Gen X replied. "But I was busy doing the wedding, so I may have missed him. Why do you think he was there?"

"Well, he tagged you in this picture, here on Facebook. So, I assumed he took the photo himself and posted it, tagging you."

As it turned out, Ethan had not been at the wedding, but had tagged Pastor Gen X in the photo because Ethan, too, was virtually 'living' the event through Mark and June's Facebook photos, photos that had been taken by various guests, on their smart phones, during and after the wedding. Just as quickly as they took the photos, the pictures were uploaded to Facebook, and accessible to both Ethan and Pastor Gen X's wife, not to mention all of Mark and June's friends and family not able to share in their special day in person.

The Board President's perspective:

"I've known June since she was little" commented Liz to her husband that evening, and I have not seen a wedding that made everyone feel so much like family in a long time. It was odd, because I really knew no one else very well. After I volunteered to help coordinate everything at church—I mean there were so many people from all over the country volunteering to help with parts of the ceremony and reception; it could have been a three-ring circus!"

"Well," said her husband Ed, "E-mail certainly makes everything easier."

"Yes," Liz agreed, "But I would have expected more difficulties because the logistics were incredible. Just getting the five clergy together early enough to make sure there would not be problems with the service was challenging enough. I mean we don't have five spaces in the parking lot reserved for clergy! They were all so accommodating though. And the food for the reception was beautifully coordinated by Chris and Jordan. I only got to know them through this wedding, and I'm so glad I did. We had a nice talk about them and their new adopted baby. I think they might come to our church and see if they are comfortable with us."

"Everyone was taking pictures with their phones, so I guess they will each have their own, and can send them to Mark and June. What a nice young man he is! June will be very happy, I think."

The Grandmother of the Groom

Grandma Patty could not wait to tell her partner about the wedding. He could not attend, of course, given his recent surgery, but he had told her to go and have a good time for both of them.

"Frank," she said, "It was so much fun!! It was just like a wedding from the Depression. Everybody brought something, and there were people there of all ages—not like that strange wedding we went to in Colorado several years ago, where there were only young people dressed in black and a few parents. Well, I mean it was like a Depression wedding in that sense, but do you know there were five ministers there, and—actually, one was a Roman Catholic priest. Can you believe it? We would never have had that in the '30's. And of course, there was a band with a drum—no organ. We wouldn't have had that, either. And everyone kept using their new phones to take pictures. We wouldn't have had that, either. And Mark and June (who looks just like your great-granddaughter Amy, I have to say) already have a house where half the wedding party stayed. Heavens! Can you imagine having a house before you are married?"

"Well, I guess it is a different world—but it certainly feels good when people come together like that!"

Appendix I:

Generational Cohorts Exercise

The goal is for participants to learn about the six cohorts and to begin to be able to place themselves and others in the appropriate cohorts. As people fill their names in the block that represents their cohort and their years of membership, they may come to see their role in the congregation as part of a larger pattern. There are no wrong answers—we are exploring these new concepts together.

Read through all the instructions first, and assemble the materials you will need. Feel free to adapt the exercise to larger or smaller groups. It is often helpful to have a practice session for key congregational leaders or the people who will facilitate the meeting first, so they not only know what to do, but understand why they are leading this exercise for others. If necessary, plan to talk about generational theory with them first, so that they do not carry any anger or resentment into the congregational meeting.

Directions for Generational Cohorts Exercise

1) Prepare a large newsprint/whiteboard version of the *Demographic Cohort Grid* (from the Introduction to this book) and a separate large newsprint/whiteboard version of the *Generational and Congregational Grid* (below). Post/display both in front of the group.
2) Assemble congregational leaders and/or those who are most active and know the most people. Introduce the Demographic Cohort concept and have everyone present tell the others which

cohort they are in by marking a large version of the *Demographic Cohort Grid* with their initials.

3) Next introduce the concept of "years of membership" and ask everyone to think about what year they joined the congregation. This may require some comparing of memories and take several minutes.

4) Move over to the *Generational and Congregational Interface Grid* and introduce it, reminding people of the concepts of "demographic cohort" and "years of membership."

5) Using markers, have each person put their names or initials in the appropriate box. In other words, if you were born in 1965, and have been a member all your life, you would go up the GenX column until you reach the 40-49 years membership row, and put your name in that box. (Clergy and staff should hold back until step 6.)

6) When everyone has done this, stop to look at the grid, and see where the clusters are. You may be surprised to see that some of the oldest members are not as chronologically old as you would expect. Some of the chronologically oldest may be among the newest members. Take some time to discuss what your own congregation's pattern is and how it plays out in your congregational life.

If you wish, a small congregation can add everyone's name. A larger congregation might want to add the names of the last three years' new members, or the names of other congregational leaders who are not present. When you are finished adding names, add the names of clergy and other program staff in a different color. Look again for clusters and see what the grid tells you.

If you repeat this with other groups within your congregation, begin each time with a fresh, unmarked copy of both grids. The results may be assembled into two summary grids for the whole congregation, but it is best simply to count the numbers in each box and enter the total, rather than put individual names or initials for everyone—unless the congregation is very small. Then clusters of high numbers can be circled for emphasis during discussion.

A blank copy of the Generational and Congregational Interface Grid appears on the next page. On the page after it is an example of a filled-out Grid with discussion.

Generational and Congregational Interface Grid

This grid shows the six cohorts and their birth years along the bottom axis, making six columns. On the left, in decade-long rows, are the number of years that persons have been members of this congregation.

Members 70+ years						
60-69 years						
50-59 years						
40-49 years						
30-39 years						
20-29 years						
10-19 years						
1-9 years						
Years as Member	Builders 1901— 1924	Silents 1925— 1945	Boomers 1946— 1960	GenXers 1961— 1981	Millennials 1982— 2000	"GenZers" 2001—

EXAMPLE FOR DISCUSSION

Generational and Congregational Interface Grid

This sample grid shows the six cohorts and their birth years along the bottom axis, making six columns. On the left, in decade-long rows, are the number of years that persons have been members of this congregation. It has been filled out as an example of a theoretical exercise.

Members						
70+ years	GH					
60-69 years						
50-59 years			AB IB			
40-49 years		IS		XW		
30-39 years	YZ	NM LM	ST HG KL BG WT			
20-29 years	UV GV	OP CD	WX ZY RQ	CB	JB AW RW	
10-19 years		FE FH		RM Pastor GenX	SM	
1-9 years	AI	QR JA BA	JI TI MN WN	TS VU	PO TO JM JR LR	EF BW KL TM EB BS
Years as Member	**Builders** 1901— 1924	**Silents** 1925— 1945	**Boomers** 1946— 1960	**GenXers** 1961— 1981	**Millennials** 1982— 2000	**"GenZers"** 2001—

Discussion

Let's say that this example was constructed on a summer Sunday morning, when Pastor GenX invited everyone present at worship to stay for iced tea and cookies and take part in a generational discovery exercise. Not everyone did, of course, but she was pleasantly surprised that there was as much interest as there was. After introducing the concepts of *generational cohort* and *years of membership,* she invited everyone present to find "their square" and put their initials in it. Last of all, she marked her own name.

Pastor GenX asked people to sit down and begin to see what the grid showed. First, she announced that there would be a plate of cookies for the "oldest member" present—that is, the person whose age and years of membership totaled the highest number. She acknowledged that the oldest member of the church, Gretchen Heinz who had celebrated her 94th birthday and her 94th year of membership, could not be with them, but Pastor GenX had taken her a plate of cookies yesterday when she visited her in the Eldercare Home. Now the question was: who gets the other plate?

Yvette Zelanie thought that she would certainly be the oldest member present, being 87 and having been a member for 30 years and she wasn't sure she wanted to claim it. But Ike Smith piped up, saying that at 66 with 52 years of membership, he had a total of 118, and he won the cookies! But just then, Al Benson said even though he and his wife Ibby are Boomers, he is actually the winner. He was 64 in April, and he had come to this church when he was five. So he has 59 years of membership for a total of 123. And his wife, Ibby, Gretchen Heinz's niece, has been a member since she was 4, and she is 62. They could do the math! Ibby blushed and said that was OK, he could have the cookies.

Pastor GenX then asked people to connect the families on the grid, and note how many generational cohorts each family represented—just among those present. The results were interesting. Queenie Righter who had offered her grandson Jim and his wife Leannie a home after they both lost their jobs last year, said she could say three, because Leannie was expecting. Nancy and Lon Miller said they are Silents, their son Rob is a GenXer, his wife Sasha is a Millennial, as is their grandson Jason, and the baby, Taddie is a GenZer—so they have five. Jenette and Tom Inverson said they had two, and that was only because Tom's mother Alice had come to live with them last year. Tewk Sahl and her partner Val Urie said they were both GenXers, and their daughter Blanche Sahl gave them two. The Wilsons, Amelia and Rich, claimed four: Rich's mother Xenia is a GenXer and Amelia's aunt and uncle, Harry and Barbara Gibson are Boomers, while their son Byron is a GenZer.

But those Bensons just grinned! Al announced that they have family members in all six cohorts: Gretchen Heinz is a Builder. Her daughter Florence Heinz, Ibby's cousin, is a Silent. Al and Ibby are Boomers. Their son Charles is a GenXer, but his wife Jayne is a Millennial, and their granddaughter Elizabeth (named for her Grandmother Ibby) is a GenZer.

"There just will be no living with you now" teased Yvette Zelanie, who had known Al since he was in his twenties. "What I want to say is that I see how much our congregation has grown since you came ten years ago, Pastor. You may not be able to take credit for the babies, but about a third of the people here have come since you began with us."

Pastor GenX thanked them all for their work, and said that she would be adding other members' names so that they had a complete picture of the congregation. What she did not mention was that except for Florence Heinz, and Rob and Sasha Miller—all of whom had family ties—only Fred Edderton, who came with his friend Opie Price, had joined and stayed during the difficult years that preceded her arrival. But the grid certainly made clear that that conflict had cost the congregation dearly.

Appendix II:

Mapping Our Congregation

 T he goal of the exercise is for participants to create a visual map (model) of their congregation, including all the people (programs) who regularly relate to it and use the buildings and grounds. They should add as much detail as they need to help everyone who looks at it to understand how the congregation fits into and relates to its community. Participants can decide who should be included and what constitutes the congregation's community.

Read through the instructions first, and assemble the materials you will need. Feel free to adapt the exercise to larger or smaller groups; but be sure that discussion groups include at least three and no more than five persons. **It is better not to have a practice session** so that no one has an already-developed map in their head before beginning. It is not necessary to have done the exercise in Appendix I before doing this exercise, and vice versa.

Directions for Congregational Mapping Exercise

A) Figure out how many break-out spaces you will need if you divide your group into small discussion groups of 3-5 persons, and locate a gathering space that is convenient to all of them.

B) Prepare enough large newsprint/posterboard sheets for every small group of 3-5 people to have two. Assemble different color post-its, colored dots, stick-on stars (or other decorative shape), colored markers, crayons, and other craft supplies sufficient for each group to have an assortment.

C) Assemble congregational leaders and fulltime staff and introduce the concept of "mapping." A roadmap is one kind of map, but there are many others. If necessary, draw a simple Venn diagram to show one kind of mental map. (See Chapter 8.) Emphasize that there are many ways of mapping or modeling information so that others can understand how the elements relate, and that each group will be free to decide how to map our congregation and its community.

D) Ask people to form groups of 3, 4 or 5 people, depending on how large the group is, and how many break-out spaces you have been able to identify. Request that they form groups based on the people present whom they know least well, of different ages and length of membership. Be sure that congregational officers and clergy are in separate groups—if clergy decide to participate, rather than observe. Tell the groups they will be presenting their maps to each other, so make them as clear and understandable as possible. No one can do this wrong, and yes, it may be hard for them to do! They will have 45 minutes to make their map.

E) Hand out work materials; send them to their break-out spaces. Go around to each group after they are settled, and be sure they understand the instructions. Ten minutes before they are to re-convene, go around and give them 10 minute warning.

F) When the whole group reconvenes, let each discussion group in turn present their map. Ask if there are any questions of fact or understanding—not comments—from other groups. After those are done, ask whether any of that particular discussion group's members have other things to add—and then move on to the rest of the groups, asking the same questions after each presentation.

G) After all discussion groups have presented their maps, send all groups back with the following instruction: *"You have now heard what each of the other groups has developed. Let go of your own group's thinking if you have heard something that has moved you to a different place. You may now modify or change your map in any way that seems right to you, including deciding that another model works better, or adopting any part of it to make your own map more Christ-like. Please take another sheet of paper/posterboard with you to revise your model as you wish."* Tell them they will have 20 minutes for this revision, and will again have to present their map/model to the assembled group.

H) When the whole group reconvenes again, have the same kind of presentation, but do it in a different group order. (If you did groups 1, 2 and 3; make it 3, 2, 1 or 3, 1, 2)

I) When all have reported, you will have similar or different models, and much to consider. Ask all present to be silent for several minutes (make this at least 3 to 5 minutes) and pray about what they have seen and heard at this meeting. Then ask whether they have anything in their hearts that needs to be said before we finish this exercise.

After everyone has said whatever they need to say, assure them that the congregational leaders will be thinking and praying about the maps that have been created. All comments will be respectfully honored, and the clergy will learn from what has been said.

J) Close with a prayer for every member of your congregation, whether present or not.

Note to leaders: You may have maps that show many versions of the same idea, differently represented, or you may have very different ideas where power resides, where the core worshipers are situated and where community exists. These are powerful clues for discerning your way forward. Below are three different maps of the same congregation developed by the same Church Board at a single session.

The Congregation as an Iceberg:
One group saw the worshipping community as the tip of an iceberg—the little visible triangle (church) being a tiny part of a huge mass of people and ministry hidden under the surface of daily life.

The Congregation as a Multi-dimensional network:
The second discussion group saw the whole congregation and community as a multi-dimensional network, linked in a thousand different ways and not separate from each other. This group had the only Millennial present.

The Congregation as a Tree:
The third group saw this congregation as a strong tree with many branches. The core worshipers formed the base and trunk of the tree, and all the branches grew from it. Different ministry and outreach programs were represented by post-its along each branch like leaves.

Acknowledgments

This book would not exist without the involvement of many people, and we want to thank them for their many insights and good advice. We have checked and rechecked, but being human, there may be errors. If there are, the errors are ours, and they are unintentional.

The Rev. Heather Patton-Graham, Lower School Chaplain, St. Alban's School, Washington, D.C. and the Rev. Alexander C. Graham, IV, A.H.C., Rector of Incarnation Holy Sacrament Church in Drexel Hill, Pennsylvania read innumerable versions of the manuscript and gave us candid GenX comments. They kept us—Boomer and Transitional—in line! The Rev. Thomas Cook, Rector of Trinity Church, Swarthmore, Pennsylvania also read an early version and tested it with his Vestry.

William Hethcock, Professor of Homiletics, Emeritus (Sewanee), read and critiqued the manuscript. His insights are largely responsible for the existence of Chapter Eight. We thank The Right Rev. Frank T. Griswold, former Presiding Bishop of the Episcopal Church for his encouragement and kind words after reading an earlier version of the book. Dr. Phyllis Tickle provided wise counsel throughout our search for the right publisher. Librarian Kay Wisniewski, at the Free Library of Philadelphia, helped greatly with early decisions about publicity and marketing.

The roots of *Congregational Connections* lie in Clergy Study Groups funded by the Continuing Education Committee of the Diocese of Pennsylvania. Participants' insights, discussion and sharing of generational issues and the conflicts within their congregations caused by misunderstandings drew us into larger questions about the six-generation society in which we now live. We thank all who were part of these groups, especially the Revs. John M. Atkins, Diana Carroll, Linda M. Kapurch, Jonathan A. Mitchican, Claire Nevin-Field, and The

Rev. Canon Mariclair Partee. We also thank St. Paul's Church, Chestnut Hill, Philadelphia, and St. Mary's Church, Ardmore, PA for hosting these clergy gatherings.

The "Congregational Moments" case studies in this book are a mixture of real congregational issues and fictional characters meant to illustrate generational challenges. In only one case is a real congregation factually described: Trinity Church in Ambler, Pennsylvania. We thank The Very Rev. David Canan and The Rev. Mary McCullough for their information about their Koinonia Service and its outcomes. There are other clergy we thank, but the stories they shared are now cloaked in changed names, details and circumstances, so we will not identify them. Except for Trinity Church's, in none of the Congregational Moments do we mean to represent a real person.

Finally, we thank Doug, Doris, Joe, Shar, Myles and Millissa for lending a hand on the cover.

Carroll Anne Sheppard and Nancy Burton Dilliplane

Chapter Notes

It Starts Here

Page 8   *Norman Rockwell, "Freedom from Want," illustration. (1943)*

Page 10   Tom Brokaw, *The Greatest Generation*, (Random House; New York; 2004)

Page 12   Gordon McDonald, *Who Stole My Church? What to Do When the Church You Love Tries to Enter the 21ˢᵗ Century (Thomas Nelson; Nashville, Tennessee; 2007)*, Chapter One.

Chapter 1. How We Got Here

Page 18   *Martin Luther King, Jr., "Social Justice and the Emerging New Age," Speech given at Western Michigan University, 1963*

Chapter 2. Six Different Cohort Experiences

Page 27   Gary L. McIntosh, *One Church, Four Generations: Understanding and Reaching All Ages in Your Church* (Baker Books: Grand Rapids, MI, 2002)

Page 30   Bob Dylan, *"The Times They Are A' Changin"*, (Columbia Records, 1964)

Page 35   Jesse Rice, *The Church of Facebook: How the Hyperconnected Are Defining Community,* (David C. Cook: Colorado Springs, CO, 2009)

Chapter 3. The Generational Divide

Page 42   Philadelphia Inquirer, *"Fewer of the Marrying Kind: The census finds wedded couples head a minority of homes nationally . . ." Page 1, (Philadelphia, PA; May 29, 2011)*

Page 43   Carol Howard Merritt, *Tribal Church: Ministering to the Missing Generation,* (The Alban Institute: Herndon, VA, 2007) pages 7-9

Chapter 4. Realities for Congregational Life

Page 50   Pew Foundation, Philadelphia Website, http.// pewsocialtrends.org *Millennials: Confident, Connected. Open to Change,* Released February 24, 2010

Page 50   *"Dustin"* Comic strip by Steve Kelley and Jeff Parker; (King Features Syndicate)

Chapter 5. Worship

Page 74   John MacDonald, *Who Stole My Church?*

Page 74   Carol Howard Merritt, *Tribal Church*

Page 75   Thomas G. Long, *Accompany Them with Singing: The Christian Funeral,* (Westminster John Knox Press: Louisville, KY, 2009)

Chapter 6. Christian Formation

Page 79   The New Revised Standard Version, copyright 1989, Division of Public Education of the National Council of Churches of Christ in the United States of America. Used by permission. All rights reserved.

Page 80   *The Book of Common Prayer and Administration of the Sacraments and Other Rites and Ceremonies of the Church,* According to the Use of The Episcopal Church, (Oxford University Press, New York, NY, 1979) page 531

Chapter 7. Programs and Space

Page 91   Sara Miles, *Take This Bread: The Spiritual Memoir of a 21ˢᵗ Century Christian,* (Ballantine Books/Random House: New York, NY, 2007)

Chapter 8. Community is Congregation

Page 101   Arlin J. Rothauge, *Sizing Up a Congregation for New Member Ministry,* (Episcopal Church Center: 1986)

Page 105   Sara Miles, *Jesus Freak: Feeding Healing Raising the Dead,* (Jossey Bass: San Francisco, CA, 2010)

Page 106   *Philadelphia Magazine,* (Philadelphia Magazine: Philadelphia, PA, March 2011 issue) Cover

Page 106   Dan Kimball, *They Like Jesus But Not the Church: Insights from Emerging Generations,* (Zondervan: Grand Rapids, MI, 2007)

Page 106   Kendra Cressy Dean, *Almost Christian: What the Faith of Our Teenagers is Telling the American Church,* (Oxford University Press: New York, NY, 2010)

Page 107   Partners for Sacred Places, Philadelphia, Website: http://sacredplaces.org

Chapter 9. The Way Forward: Love

Page 113   Phyllis Tickle, *The Great Emergence: How Cristianity is Changing and Why,* (Baker Books; Grand Rapids, MI; 2008) Chapter One.

Works Cited and Suggestions for Further Reading

Diana Butler Bass; **Christianity for the Rest of Us: How the Neighborhood Church is Transforming the Faith;** Alban Institute; Herndon, VA 2007

Rob Bell; **Velvet Elvis: Repainting the Christian Faith;** Zondervan; 2005.

The Book of Common Prayer and Administration of the Sacraments and Other Rites and Ceremonies of the Church, According to the Use of The Episcopal Church; Oxford University Press; New York, NY; 1979

Laurene Beth Bowers; **Designing Contemporary Congregations: Strategies to Attract Those under 50;** Pilgrim Press; Cleveland, Ohio; 2008

Thomas E. Bridenthal; **Christian Households: The Sanctification of Nearness**; Wipf & Stock Publishers; 2004.

Tom Brokaw; **The Greatest Generation;** Random House; New York; 2004

Colleen Carroll; **The New Faithful: Why Young Adults Are Embracing Christian Orthodoxy;** Loyola Press; 2002

Jackson Carroll; **Mainline to the Future: Congregations for the 21st Century**; Westminster John Knox Press; 2000.

Graeme Codrington and Sue Grant Marshall; **Mind the Gap;** Penguin Books; 2004.

Kendra Cressy Dean; **Almost Christian: What the Faith of Our Teenagers is Telling the American Church;** Oxford University Press, USA; 2010.

Bob Dylan; *"The Times They Are A' Changin";* Columbia Records, 1964

Eric Greenberg, Karl Weber and Designpool; **Generation We: How Millennial Youth are Taking Over America and Changing Our World Forever;** Pachatusan; 2008

Edward H. Hammett and James R. Pierce; **Reaching People Under 40 and Keeping People Over 60;** Chalice Press; St. Louis, MO; 2007

Neil Howe, William Strauss and R. J. Matson; **Millennials Rising: The Next Great Generation; Vintage;** 2000.

Dan Kimball; **They Like Jesus But Not the Church: Insights from Emerging Generations;** Zondervan; 2007.

Martin Luther King, Jr. **"Social Justice and the Emerging New Age,"** speech given at Western Michigan University, 1963

David Kinnaman and Gabe Lyons; **UnChristian—What a New Generation Really Thinks About Christianity;** Baker Books; Grand Rapids, MI; 2007

Thomas G. Long; **Accompany Them with Singing: The Christian Funeral;** Westminster John Knox Press; Louisville, KY; 2009

Gordon MacDonald; **Who Stole My Church: What to Do When the Church You Love Tries to Enter the 21st Century;** Thomas Nelson; Nashville, Tennessee; 2007

Beth Maynard: **How to Evangelize a GenX-er (NOT);** Forward Movement Publications; Cincinnati, Oh 2001

Brian McClaren; **Everything Must Change: Jesus, Global Crises and a Revolution of Hope;** Thomas Nelson; Nashville, TN; 2007.

Gary L. McIntosh; **One Church, Four Generations: Understanding and Reaching All Ages in Your Church;** Baker Books, 2002.

Carol Howard Merritt; **Tribal Church: Ministering to the Missing Generation;** The Alban Institute; Herndon; VA 2007

Sara Miles; **Take This Bread: The Spiritual Memoir of a 21ˢᵗ Century Christian;** Ballantine Books/Random House; New York, NY; 2007

Jesus Freak: Feeding, Healing, Raising the Dead; Jossey Bass; San Francisco; 2010

Bonnie Miller-McLemore; **In the Midst of Chaos: Caring for Children as Spiritual Practice;** John Wiley & Sons; San Francisco; 2006

Craig Kennet Miller and MaryJane Pierce Norton; **Making God Real for a New Generation: Ministry with Millennials Born from 1982 to 1999;** Discipleship Resources, 2003.

Lisa Orrell; **Millennials Incorporated: The Big Business of Recruiting, Managing and Retaining the World's New Generation of Young Professionals;** Intelligent Women Publishing; 2ⁿᵈ Edition, 2008

Partners for Sacred Places, Philadelphia: **Website: http:// sacredplaces. org**

Pew Foundation, Philadelphia: **Website: http.//pewsocialtrends.org** See especially: *Millennials: Confident, Connected. Open to Change,* Released February 24, 2010

Philadelphia Inquirer, article: Fewer of the Marrying Kind: The census finds wedded couples head a minority of homes nationally and in PA. and just 51% in N.J.; Philadelphia, PA; May 29, 2011

Christian Piatt and Amy Piatt; **My Space to Sacred Space: God for a New Generation;** Chalice Press, 2007.

Sam Anthony Portaro; **Mind the Gap: Forming a New Generation of Leadership for the Church;** Forward Movement Publications; 2003

Jesse Rice; **The Church of Facebook: How the Hyperconnected Are Defining Community**; David C. Cook; Colorado Springs, CO; 2009

Arlin J. Rothauge; **Sizing Up a Congregation for New Member Ministry;** Episcopal Church Center; 1986

Sara Wenger Shenk; **Thank You for Asking: Conversing With Young Adults about the Future Church;** Herald Press; Scottsdale, PA 2005

William Strauss and Neil Howe; **Generations: The History of America's Future, 1584 to 2069;** William Morrow, New York; 1991

Phyllis Tickle; **The Great Emergence: How Christianity is Changing and Why;** Baker Books; Grand Rapids, Michigan; 2008

Howard Vanderwell, Editor; **The Church of All Ages: Generations Worshiping Together;** Alban Institute; Herndon, VA; 2008.

Ron Zemke, Claire Raines and Bob Filipczak; **Generations at Work: Managing the Clash of Veterans, Boomers, Xers and Nexters in Your Workplace;** AMACOM; 1999

SWPA Synod Resource Center
9625 Perry Highway
Pittsburgh, PA 15237

24437771R00074

Made in the USA
Lexington, KY
24 July 2013